Collective Worship for
PRIMARY SCHOOLS

Text copyright © Helen Jaeger 2016
The author asserts the moral right
to be identified as the author of this work

Published by
The Bible Reading Fellowship
15 The Chambers, Vineyard
Abingdon OX14 3FE
United Kingdom
Tel: +44 (0)1865 319700
Email: enquiries@brf.org.uk
Website: www.brf.org.uk
BRF is a Registered Charity

ISBN 978 0 85746 459 0

First published 2016
10 9 8 7 6 5 4 3 2 1 0
All rights reserved

Acknowledgements
Unless otherwise stated, scripture quotations are taken from The Holy Bible, New International Version (Anglicised edition) copyright © 1979, 1984, 2011 by Biblica. Used by permission of Hodder & Stoughton Publishers, a Hachette UK company. All rights reserved. 'NIV' is a registered trademark of Biblica. UK trademark number 1448790.

Scripture quotations taken from the Holy Bible, New Living Translation, copyright © 1996, 2004, 2007, 2013. Used by permission of Tyndale House Publishers, Inc., Carol Stream, Illinois 60188. All rights reserved.

Scripture quotations from The New Revised Standard Version of the Bible, Anglicised edition, copyright © 1989, 1995 by the Division of Christian Education of the National Council of the Churches of Christ in the United States of America. Used by permission. All rights reserved.

Cover photo: © David Lund

Every effort has been made to trace and contact copyright owners for material used in this resource. We apologise for any inadvertent omissions or errors, and would ask those concerned to contact us so that full acknowledgement can be made in the future.

A catalogue record for this book is available from the British Library

Printed by Gutenberg Press, Tarxien, Malta

Collective Worship for PRIMARY SCHOOLS

50 easy-to-use Bible-based assembly outlines for teaching essential life skills

Helen Jaeger

Important Information

Photocopying permission

The right to photocopy material in *Collective Worship for Primary Schools* is granted for the pages that contain the photocopying clause 'Reproduced with permission from *Collective Worship for Primary Schools* by Helen Jaeger (Barnabas in Schools, 2016)', so long as reproduction is for use in a teaching situation by the original purchaser. The right to photocopy material is not granted for anyone other than the original purchaser without written permission from BRF.

The Copyright Licensing Agency (CLA)

If you are resident in the UK and you have a photocopying licence with the Copyright Licensing Agency (CLA) please check the terms of your licence. If your photocopying request falls within the terms of your licence, you may proceed without seeking further permission. If your request exceeds the terms of your CLA licence, please contact the CLA directly with your request. Copyright Licensing Agency, Saffron House, 6–10 Kirby Street, London EC1N 8TS. Telephone 020 7400 3100; fax 020 7400 3101; email cla@cla.co.uk; website www.cla.co.uk. The CLA will provide photocopying authorisation and royalty fee information on behalf of BRF.

BRF is a Registered Charity (No. 233280)

Contents

Suggested ways to use this book 7
1 Anti-bullying 8
2 Asking for forgiveness 9
3 Being courageous 10
4 Being friends 11
5 Being good listeners 12
6 Being inclusive 13
7 Being kind in what we say 14
8 Being kind to each other 15
9 Being ourselves 16
10 Being outdoors 17
11 Being patient 18
12 Being thankful 19
13 Caring for each other 21
14 Celebrating 22
15 Copying good behaviour 23
16 Falling out and making up 24
17 Family 25
18 Follow the star 26
19 Gifts and talents 27
20 Going on holiday 28
21 Good choices 29
22 Growing and learning 30
23 Home 31
24 Keeping going 32
25 Knowing all about you 33
26 Laughing is good for you 34
27 Learning from each other 35
28 Looking forward 36
29 Making mistakes 37
30 Meeting angels 38
31 More than enough 39

32	Mother's Day: mums and carers	40
33	Mother's Day: people who help	41
34	Planting seeds	42
35	Prejudice	43
36	Respecting others	44
37	Rest and relaxation	45
38	Role models	46
39	Saying goodbye	47
40	Setting a good example	48
41	Sharing together	49
42	Sharing worries	50
43	Staying healthy	51
44	Stronger together	52
45	Superheroes	53
46	The importance of books	54
47	The nativity	55
48	Try something new	56
49	Working together	57
50	World feasts	58

Appendix A
Christian festivals and seasons through the year 59

Appendix B
Significant events in the school year 62

Suggested ways to use this book

Each assembly outline in this book can be used individually as a stand-alone resource, or, where the school is focusing on a particular theme for longer than just assembly time, it can be combined with other ideas. The assembly themes are presented in alphabetical order, but you will find at the end of this book two appendices that show which assemblies might fit with (1) Christian seasons or (2) events that are significant to the school during the year. Since some themes will recur in the life of a school and will therefore receive ongoing emphasis (for example, kindness, or the Christmas story), more than one outline has been provided for these themes. This allows choice and enables different treatments over a number of years, possibly in conjunction with other resources.

Each assembly outline is divided into seven sections, as listed below. All the outlines follow exactly the same format, for ease of use, but different elements are optional. Your choices will depend on the type of assembly you want to offer, the time and space you have available and the children you are going to be with.

- **Before you start:** This section highlights any resources or materials that you'll need to bring with you or that need to be made or prepared beforehand.
- **Opener:** Each opening activity, game or story script has been designed to link with the theme of the assembly. You'll often need volunteers to take part: try to choose people with a range of ages, talents and abilities, being inclusive and representing all the different classes and Key Stages present.
- **Thought for the day:** Each small 'Thought for the day' ties in with the opening activity, summarises a key idea and leads on to the Bible story, meditation and prayer.
- **What the Bible says:** Key Bible stories or short verses linked to the theme are included in full, with their references. You could print out these passages and ask a child to read them out or you could read them out yourself. Where necessary, feel free to expand on the points in the Bible verse or story, ensuring that the children understand what the passage means as a whole, as well as any difficult words or unfamiliar concepts. You may like to supplement the Bible stories and verses with art or other visual aids. There are plenty of materials online that you could use, but always make sure that they are copyright-free and available for public use.
- **Questions:** You can use the questions to encourage further interaction or as a basis for your own summary of the biblical information.
- **Reflection:** Having a quiet time of reflection allows the children to assimilate what they've seen and learned, as well as offering them a private space in which to make a response.
- **Prayer:** You can end the assembly with the prayer provided or with one of your own. You may wish to light a candle at this point.

It is a good idea to start and end the assembly with some music playing quietly in the background. This sets the tone and helps the children to recognise the beginning and end of the activities. It also encourages responsive listening and good behaviour from the children as they enter and leave the assembly.

If you are using technological resources such as an overhead projector, internet, visualiser or laptop, check that everything is up and running smoothly before you start.

Have fun and enjoy your assemblies as a time of learning and interaction!

1 Anti-bullying

Before you start

Bring to the assembly two cans of squirty cream, a waterproof tablecloth, and aprons for the children. You will need two tables. You could also download a picture of Jesus and the lepers, to provide a visual focus for the Bible story.

Opener: Squirty cream relay

Choose two teams of three or four children each. Line up each team at a short distance from a table and give them each a can of squirty cream. Tell them they are going to play 'squirty cream relay'. Each player must run to the table, squeeze out a line of cream on to it, run back to their team and hand the can to the next player. Set a time limit that fits with the length of your assembly. When the time is up, see which team has managed to squirt out the most cream.

Declare the winning team. Now tell the children that they must play Round 2: this time they must get all the cream back into their can. Say, 'What do you mean, you can't get it all back in?' Ask the teams to sit down.

Thought for the day

If we bully someone and regret it later, it's like trying to get the cream back into the can. If we do or say something hurtful to another person, we can't easily take it back.

What the Bible says

Jesus and a man with a skin disease

A man with leprosy came and knelt in front of Jesus, begging to be healed. 'If you are willing, you can heal me and make me clean,' he said. Moved with compassion, Jesus reached out and touched him. 'I am willing,' he said. 'Be healed!' Instantly the leprosy disappeared, and the man was healed.

MARK 1:40–42 (NLT)

Explain that, in Bible times, having leprosy was one of the worst things that could happen to you. People avoided you and didn't want to be near you.

Questions

- How was being a leper in Jesus' time a bit like being bullied?
- How did Jesus let the leper know he cared about him?
- How can we reach out to other people?

Reflection

Ask the children to close their eyes and think quietly about what they've heard today.

Prayer

Thank you, Jesus, that you love and accept everyone. Help us to be more loving and caring to everyone around us, just as you were—and especially to those who may feel on the outside. Amen

2 Asking for forgiveness

Before you start

Hand out a sheet of paper and a pencil to every child as they come into assembly.

Opener: Drawing a mistake

Ask the children if they've ever made a mistake. What was it? What happened and how did they feel about it? You can ask volunteers to share publicly if they feel comfortable to do so.

Now invite the children to write or draw a picture of a time when they made a mistake. You could give examples, such as:

- not listening to Mum or Dad
- forgetting what they were meant to be doing in school
- losing their PE kit
- not following instructions
- not paying attention to directions

Ask for volunteers to explain what they did to put the situation right—for example, owning up, saying sorry, or doing something nice for another person. Then ask them how they felt about it—good, happy, or relieved?

Finally, invite all the children to imagine they have said sorry for the mistake that they've written or drawn. Ask them to scrunch up their piece of paper and be ready to put it in a bin on the way out of assembly. Explain that that's what saying sorry and being forgiven is all about. It's a chance to bin our mistakes.

Thought for the day

When we do something wrong, we feel bad, but when we say sorry and put it right, we usually feel a lot better.

What the Bible says

Jesus says we must forgive

Then Peter came to Jesus and asked, 'Lord, how many times shall I forgive my brother or sister who sins against me? Up to seven times?' Jesus answered, 'I tell you, not seven times, but seventy times seven.'

MATTHEW 18:21–22

Questions

- How much did Peter think he should forgive— a little or a lot?
- How much did Jesus think he should forgive— a little or a lot?
- Why do you think Jesus told his friend, Peter, that it's important to forgive others?

Reflection

Ask the children to close their eyes and think quietly about what they've heard today.

Prayer

Thank you, Jesus, that when we make a mistake and say sorry, that's it—it's over. Thank you that you don't keep on reminding us about our mistakes and that you tell everyone how important forgiveness is. Thank you for the gift of forgiveness. Amen

---

Reproduced with permission from *Collective Worship for Primary Schools* by Helen Jaeger (Barnabas in Schools, 2016) www.barnabasinschools.org.uk

3 Being courageous

Before you start

Make a large cut-out figure that looks scary or has words like 'fear' and 'worry' written on it. Prop it up in the assembly hall so that it stands upright but could fall over if someone threw a beanbag at it hard enough. Have a stack of beanbags ready.

Prepare a slideshow presentation with images of people standing up for human rights and historical figures who have been courageous.

Opener: Beanbag busted

Ask the children, 'What is courage and what does it do?' Answers could include: courage is bravery; it helps us face our worries and fears, helps us to stand up for what we believe in, helps us to protect other people or animals, helps us to try new things, and helps us to grow and learn.

Ask the children, 'When was the last time you had to be brave? Where were you and what did you do? Was it hard or easy to be brave?'

Explain that your cut-out figure is the figure of fear, and it's really scary, but it can be beaten. What would you need to beat it with? (Courage)

As each child gives an answer, invite them to throw a beanbag at the figure of fear until it's knocked over.

Now ask the children to imagine what it would be like if you lived in a place where your beliefs were not allowed, and where there was a danger that you could be beaten up or thrown into prison if you stood up for your beliefs, even if they were good beliefs and the things you wanted were for the good of everyone.

Say that there have been many people in history who have stood up for what they believed in, because they wanted the world to be a better place, even though they were threatened and even killed. Can the children think of anyone like this? Show them your slideshow of famous courageous people.

Tell the children that there are still places in the world today where people need to have courage to stand up for what is right under persecution.

Thought for the day

We may not have to be courageous in big ways, but we can stand up for what is right—maybe if there is a fight in the playground or if a teacher asks us to tell the truth about something that has happened. We may need to be brave, perhaps if we find a lesson difficult or if a friend falls out with us. Invite the children to be brave today and not to be beaten by fear.

What the Bible says

God chooses a courageous leader

Moses was the leader of a big group of people from Israel. He led the Israelites out from slavery in Egypt to a new land that God wanted to give to them. But Moses was getting old, so he needed to appoint a new leader. God wanted a man called Joshua to lead the Israelites into the country he was giving them.

Then Moses summoned Joshua and said to him in the presence of all Israel, 'Be strong and courageous, for you must go with this people into the land that the Lord swore to their ancestors to give them, and you must divide it among them as their inheritance. The Lord himself goes before you and will be with you; he will never leave you nor forsake you. Do not be afraid; do not be discouraged.'

DEUTERONOMY 31:7–8

Questions

- What was Joshua about to do?
- How do you think he was feeling?
- Why did Moses tell Joshua he didn't need to be afraid?

Reflection

Ask the children to close their eyes and think quietly about what they've heard today.

Prayer

Thank you, Jesus, that you help us to do things that are difficult or scary. Thank you that you are much bigger than fear and that if we need help, we only have to ask you to help us. Help us to be brave and to stand up for what is right. Please give courage to people who are standing up for what is right in our world today. Amen

4 Being friends

Before you start

Bring to assembly some cut-out figures of people on coloured paper and a board to stick them on.

Opener: What makes a good friend?

Ask the children if they know what these words mean: *mik* (Albanian); *tomdachi* (Japanese); *jingu* (Korean); *amic* (Italian); *rafiki* (Swahili); *ami* (French); *amigo* (Spanish).

What about 'pal', 'mate' or 'chum'?

Explain that today's assembly is all about friendship. Ask the children, 'What is a good friend like?' Answers could include the following:

- fun
- kind
- sharing
- gentle
- reliable
- there for you
- on your side, especially when things go wrong
- helpful
- forgiving
- patient
- likes you

As the children come up with answers, write them on to your coloured paper people.

Now explain that friendships can sometimes be a bit difficult. Maybe there are misunderstandings, and people fall out or stop getting along. Ask the children how you can sort things out if you fall out with a friend. Answers could include: talk about it together; get another friend or adult to help you sort out the problem; say sorry.

Say, too, that sometimes we don't know how to make new friends or we feel shy about getting to know someone.

Thought for the day

Someone once said that the best way to make friends or keep friends is to be a good friend. Now we have some ideas about how to do that.

What the Bible says

Why friends are good for us

A friend loves at all times, and a brother is born for a time of adversity.

PROVERBS 17:17

Explain that 'adversity' means tough times.

Questions

- What is special about a good friend?
- How can you be a good friend, according to these words from the Bible?
- What do you like about your best friends?

Reflection

Ask the children to close their eyes and think quietly about what they've heard today.

Prayer

Thank you, Jesus, that you give us friends. Thank you that, if we ask you, you will be our friend too. Help us to be good friends to each other, today and every day. Amen

5 Being good listeners

Before you start

Bring to assembly a 'talking stick'. You can make one by decorating an ordinary short stick with fabric, feathers, beads, bells, leaves, ribbon, cord and string, in whatever design you like.

Also prepare three cards with the following words printed on them:

> 1 I told you it was time to go to bed! Why are you still up? You're so naughty and you never listen to what you're told to do. I'm tired of telling you to go to bed. Why can't you be like your sister and get to bed on time, without us having to nag you?
>
> 2 There was a spider under my bed. I was really scared and I started to cry. He came into my bedroom to see what the problem was. He told me not to worry and that he'd sort the problem out. He found a book and got the spider to climb on to it, then he opened my window and let the spider out.
>
> 3 I was just trying to help my sister. I heard her crying and I went to see what the problem was. There was a spider in her room and she was scared. So I found my book and got the spider on to it. Then we opened the bedroom window and let it out. I wasn't being naughty!

Opener: The taking-turns talking stick

Ask three children who like acting to come to the front. Give each of them one of the numbered cards. When they've read through their card, ask them, on the count of three, to read out what's written on their card, all at the same time, confidently and loudly. It will probably be impossible to work out what each speaker is saying.

Now ask the rest of the children what was wrong. Was it easy or hard to hear what was being said? Why? What would have made it better?

Introduce your 'talking stick'. Explain that some people use a 'talking stick' when they are discussing things in a group. Only the person holding the stick is allowed to speak, so that everyone gets heard. Now hand the talking stick to the child holding card 1 and ask them to read it out. Pass the stick to the second child, who reads card 2, and finally to the third child, who reads card 3.

Ask the other children if the readings made sense this time. Explain that it's just as important to listen as it is to talk. Invite them to practise both listening and speaking for the rest of the day.

Thought for the day

If we speak too soon, without listening, we may get the wrong idea. It's just as important to listen as it is to say something, even if we're right.

What the Bible says

It's important to listen as well as speak

My dear brothers and sisters, take note of this: everyone should be quick to listen, slow to speak and slow to become angry.

JAMES 1:19

Questions

- Why is it good to listen?
- Why do you think we should be 'slow to speak', as the reading suggests?
- How can we try not to get angry quickly?

Reflection

Ask the children to close their eyes and think quietly about what they've heard today.

Prayer

Thank you, Jesus, that you listened to everyone who came to you, and you gave them advice based on what they said. Help us to listen to each other. We all need to take turns to speak and listen. Help us to be caring to others like that today. Amen

6 Being inclusive

Before you start

Prepare three presents, one beautifully wrapped (with expensive-looking shiny paper, ribbons, cellophane and tags), one not quite so well wrapped (neatly, but without the extra sparkle), and one very shabbily wrapped (just in newspaper or kitchen roll and string).

In the expensive-looking wrapping, place a very cheap gift; in the neat but plain wrapping, put an average-quality gift; and in the shabby wrapping, place the most valuable gift.

Opener: Choose the best gift

Show the presents to the children and make a big deal of how nice the expensively wrapped present looks, how good the not-so-well-wrapped gift looks, too, and how awful the badly wrapped present looks.

Invite a child to come out and choose a present, then another and finally a third. Now ask them to open their gifts and show everyone what is inside. Are they surprised by what they find?

Explain that it's not always how something looks that tells you what it's worth. Sometimes very simple, plain wrappings can contain the best gifts. It's always good not to judge something by outside appearances, because you don't know what's inside.

Ask the children to return the gifts to the assembly leader.

Thought for the day

You can't always tell what someone is like, just by looking at them. It's important not to judge things based on appearances, especially people. Everyone has hidden strengths and good qualities.

What the Bible says

Walking with humility

He has shown you, O mortal, what is good. And what does the Lord require of you? To act justly and to love mercy and to walk humbly with your God.

MICAH 6:8

Questions

- According to this reading, what three things should we try to do?
- What would be some examples of doing these things?
- What do you think 'humbly' means?

Reflection

Ask the children to close their eyes and think quietly about what they've heard today.

Prayer

Thank you, Jesus, that you love all of us, no matter what we look like. You aren't bothered by appearances. You look at our hearts. Help us to be loving and kind today, just as you are. Amen

7 Being kind in what we say

Before you start

Bring to assembly a container filled with small items—for example, 'hundreds and thousands', silver balls, dried beans, staples or giftwrap confetti.

Opener: Spilling the beans

Ask a volunteer to come to the front and open the container. Invite them to empty it out in front of them. Now ask them to pick up every single bit that dropped out of the container and put it back inside. You could set a time limit—for example, two minutes.

When the time is up, have a look to see if every piece has been picked up. Hold up any bits you find, to show that not everything has gone back into the container.

Thank your volunteer and ask them to sit back down. Now ask the children some of the following questions.

- Have you ever used words in an unkind way to hurt someone's feelings?
- What does it mean to say that someone gossips?
- What does the phrase 'It's not what you say, but how you say it' mean?
- Have you heard the saying 'Sticks and stones will break my bones, but words will never hurt me'? Do you think it's true or not?
- If you heard someone saying something unkind about a friend of yours, what would you do?

Thought for the day

Explain that when we say unkind things about other people or spread rumours, it's very difficult to take our words back. They are a bit like the things that came out of the container—easy to spill but difficult to clear up—so it's best not to say those things in the first place.

What the Bible says

What not to do

There are six things the Lord hates, seven that are detestable to him: haughty eyes, a lying tongue, hands that shed innocent blood, a heart that devises wicked schemes, feet that are quick to rush into evil, a false witness who pours out lies and a person who stirs up conflict in the community.

PROVERBS 6:16–19

Questions

- What sorts of things are on the list of things God doesn't like?
- Which ones involve saying bad things?
- Do you think we should take this list seriously? Why or why not?

Reflection

Ask the children to close their eyes and think quietly about what they've heard today.

Prayer

Thank you, Jesus, that you show us the best way to live. We're sorry for all the times we've said something unkind or untrue about someone else. Help us to be kind and thoughtful in everything we say and do. Amen

8 Being kind to each other

Before you start

Bring to assembly a colourful pinboard, coloured sheets of paper and marker pens.

Opener: Random acts of kindness

Create a 'random acts of kindness' board. Ask the children for suggestions of what could be a random act of kindness—that is, something kind that you do for someone else, just because you want to be kind, and not because they ask for it.

Examples might include:

- letting someone go in front of you in a queue
- giving a friend a random hug, without being asked
- offering to clear someone's lunch tray away
- smiling at everyone

Invite the children to choose just one of the items on their list and to do it today.

Thought for the day

We don't always have to be asked, to be kind. We can be kind to each other just because we want to be. As well as making someone else feel good, it usually makes us feel good, too.

What the Bible says

How to be kind

Be kind and compassionate to one another, forgiving each other, just as in Christ God forgave you.

EPHESIANS 4:32

Questions

- What sort of behaviour isn't kind?
- How can we go out of our way to be especially kind to each other?
- Is kindness just about being nice or doing helpful things?

Reflection

Ask the children to close their eyes and think quietly about what they've heard today.

Prayer

Thank you, Jesus, that you are so kind. You look after us and care for us. You think kindness is a really good thing. Help us to be kind to each other—to lend a hand, an ear, a smile or a kind word. Amen

Reproduced with permission from *Collective Worship for Primary Schools* by Helen Jaeger (Barnabas in Schools, 2016) www.barnabasinschools.org.uk

9 Being ourselves

Before you start

Prepare eight separate pieces of card, with the name of a different animal written on each one—for example, gorilla, lion, mouse, cat, dog, snake, kangaroo and goldfish.

Opener: Animal antics

Invite eight volunteers to come out to the front. Hand them each a card and ask them to act out what's on it, one at a time, without telling anyone or showing the card. Tell them they can use actions and noises and move around the hall wherever they like.

Allow a few minutes for each actor to get into the role and for the rest of the children to enjoy the display. Then ask the volunteer to return to the front of the hall, still in their role as the animal they were given.

Ask the rest of the children if they can guess what animal each person was acting out. As each animal is correctly guessed, the volunteers can return to their places.

Now ask how easy they think it is to act out the part of an animal. It may be easy for a few minutes, but imagine if you had to keep it up for a whole day or week, or even a month.

Thought for the day

Christians believe that God made some amazing animals, which are able to do lots of funny things, even some things that humans can't do. They believe that God also made humans. Not only that, but every single human being is unique.

There is no one quite like each one of us, and God loves us to be ourselves—not like anyone else and not like a gorilla, lion or snake (although it's fun to act those parts sometimes).

What the Bible says

In the Bible there is a book of psalms, which are songs or prayers to God. In one psalm, the writer says this:

For you created my inmost being; you knit me together in my mother's womb. I praise you because I am fearfully and wonderfully made; your works are wonderful, I know that full well.

PSALM 139:13–14

Questions

- What does the psalm writer say about how God made us?
- According to this psalm, how well does God know us, inside and out?
- If God knows and loves us, how might this make us feel?

Reflection

Ask the children to close their eyes and think quietly about what they've heard today.

Prayer

Thank you, Jesus, that each one of us is unique. Thank you that you made every person just the way you wanted them to be. Some of us are tall, some of us are short, some of us are funny and some of us are serious. It's good to be ourselves. Help us to appreciate ourselves and each other today. Amen

10 Being outdoors

Before you start

Prepare a large rainbow using different coloured card. Bring to assembly a range of large pieces of card, marker pens and sticky tack. You may also like to have some visual aids prepared to help the children think of different coloured things.

Opener: The amazing colours of nature

Ask the children to think about their favourite things in nature. Explain that you are going to fill your rainbow with beautiful things that you can find outside in nature, from the top of the rainbow to the bottom. Ask them to think first of things that are red, then orange, then yellow, green, blue, indigo and violet. Answers might include the blue sky, the green grass, a yellow insect, a violet plant, an orange sunset or a purple flower. Continue until your rainbow is full of ideas.

Thought for the day

Isn't it amazing that the world is such a colourful, beautiful place? Encourage the children to look out for colourful things outside today, perhaps at break time or on their way home.

What the Bible says

The world tells us about God

The heavens declare the glory of God; the skies proclaim the work of his hands. Day after day they pour forth speech; night after night they reveal knowledge. They have no speech, they use no words; no sound is heard from them. Yet their voice goes out into all the earth, their words to the ends of the world. In the heavens God has pitched a tent for the sun. It is like a bridegroom coming out of his chamber, like a champion rejoicing to run his course. It rises at one end of the heavens and makes its circuit to the other; nothing is deprived of its warmth.

PSALM 19:1–6

Questions

- If God made the sky and sun and stars, what could these things tell us about their creator?
- What is your favourite thing in nature? Is it a plant or tree or animal or bird? Why?

Reflection

Ask the children to close their eyes and think quietly about what they've heard today.

Prayer

Thank you, Jesus, for the beautiful gift of creation. Thank you for the sky, the sun, the grass, the wind, the air we breathe and the food we eat. Thank you for all the animals and insects. Thank you that the world is so lovely to look at and to live in. We appreciate your world! Amen

> Optional: Sing a song, like 'All things bright and beautiful'.

11 Being patient

Before you start

Bring some colourful plastic drinking straws (not the bendy kind) and some raw potatoes. You will also need a potato with a straw already pushed through it. (Making one in advance gives you a chance to check your own technique, the strength of your straws and whether your potatoes are soft enough.)

To push a straw through a potato successfully, you must know the right technique. First, place a thumb over the end closest to you. Now jab the straw quickly at the potato in one swift move. This should ensure that you can puncture the potato. If you want to fill the whole straw with potato, remove the straw, turn it upside down, again put your thumb over the top end and jab it into the potato as before. (If you don't cover the end of the straw, it won't pierce the potato.)

Opener: Potato challenge

Hold up a potato and a straw. Ask the children if they think the straw can go through the potato. Some of the children are likely to say 'yes', some will say 'no' and others will be doubtful.

Invite some volunteers forward to have a go.

It's likely that, unless the children know the right technique for pushing the straw through the potato, they won't be able to do it—at least, not on their first attempt. Give the children time to have several attempts. You may like to invite other volunteers forward to have a go as well.

If a child does manage to do it successfully, ask them to demonstrate how they did it.

Now show them the potato you've prepared with a straw through it. Tell the children it is possible, and demonstrate how to do it. You could turn the same straw around and insert it twice into the same potato, so that you end up with a straw almost full of potato.

Ask the children if they spotted what exactly you were doing and how you did it. If they don't understand, explain clearly. Let your volunteers have another go and see if they can get it right.

Finish by congratulating any children who managed to puncture their potato, but also congratulate those who didn't succeed. Tell them that although you were looking for someone to be successful, you were also watching to see who would be patient and not give up.

Thought for the day

Although it's good to know how to do things, being successful isn't always about having all the answers. It's more often about being patient and persevering.

What the Bible says

Simeon's patience is rewarded

Now there was a man in Jerusalem called Simeon, who was righteous and devout. He was waiting for the consolation of Israel, and the Holy Spirit was on him. It had been revealed to him by the Holy Spirit that he would not die before he had seen the Lord's Messiah. Moved by the Spirit, he went into the temple courts. When the parents brought in the child Jesus to do for him what the custom of the Law required, Simeon took him in his arms and praised God, saying:

'Sovereign Lord, as you have promised, you may now dismiss your servant in peace. For my eyes have seen your salvation, which you have prepared in the sight of all nations: a light for revelation to the Gentiles, and the glory of your people Israel.'

The child's father and mother marvelled at what was said about him.

LUKE 2:25–33

Questions

- What did Simeon do, and why?
- How do you feel when you finally get something you've waited a long time for?
- What can help us be patient?

Reflection

Ask the children to close their eyes and think quietly about what they've heard today.

Prayer

Thank you, Jesus, for the gift of patience. Thank you that, with patience, we're able to do a lot more than we think we can. Thank you that you are always patient with us. Amen

12 Being thankful

Before you start

Bring to assembly a copy of the story below. You may want to invite some children to act it out as you read. If so, provide some props to help them—for example, a toothbrush and toothpaste, a bowl of cornflakes, a school bag, a computer game, and so on.

Opener: Miserable and happy

Read out the following story.

Have you heard about the miserable boy? Each morning he woke up and thought about all the bad things that were going to happen that day. Grumpily, he got out of bed. Brrr, the floor was so cold! He stumbled to the bathroom and brushed his teeth—urgh! Next he got his breakfast—boring old cornflakes, again! After that, he went to switch on the TV, but found his sister was already watching it. 'Another one of her stupid programmes,' he thought to himself and wandered miserably off.

The boy climbed back up to his bedroom and got dressed for school. Yes, it was going to be another boring and miserable day!

When he got to school, one of his friends called him over to play football, but the miserable boy was in no mood to play games. 'I'm not playing if Sam's playing,' he said and walked off. The miserable boy also thought it was starting to drizzle—yuk!

When the boy went into his classroom, he could see some of his friends talking and laughing in the corner. 'They're probably talking and laughing about me,' he said to himself and decided not to join them. The rest of that day, the boy was—guess what? Miserable! Same boring lessons, same packed lunch, same after-school activities. He could hardly wait to get home, but even when he got home it was the same boring programmes on TV and the same stupid computer games, and then eating tea with his sister, mum and dad, talking about the same rubbish things.

Finally, the miserable boy got to the end of the day. He brushed his teeth again, dumped his clothes in the laundry basket and said goodnight to his sister, mum and dad—miserably. He was almost relieved to get into bed—but he wasn't really, because going to sleep was really boring and miserable too. Wasn't it?

Now did you hear about the thankful girl?

Each morning she woke up and thought about all the good things that were going to happen that day. Happily, she got out of bed. Brrr, the floor was cold, but it was fun because it made her toes tingle! She skipped to the bathroom and brushed her teeth. Ooh, now that was better, they felt really clean! Next she got her breakfast. Yummy cornflakes again, her favourite! After that, she went to switch on the TV, but found her sister was already watching something. The programme looked like fun, so she stayed to watch a bit of it, having a cuddle with her sister.

Then the girl ran back up to her bedroom and got dressed for school. Mum had used that washing powder she liked, and her clothes smelled lovely!

When she got to school, one of her friends called her over to play, and she dropped her bag, saying, 'Just coming!' Soon it looked like it was going to drizzle. The happy girl thought about how much the grass and flowers would like the rain, and it probably meant there would be 'wet play' at break time with her friends, so they could play some board games.

When the happy girl went into her classroom, she could see some of her friends talking and laughing in the corner. 'I bet they're telling that great joke I heard yesterday,' she said to herself and went over to join them. The rest of that day, the girl was—guess what? Happy! She tried her best in all her lessons, enjoyed her packed lunch and had fun in her after-school activities. She even enjoyed it when home time came—she couldn't wait to see her sister, mum and dad. When she got home, she played a few games on the computer, watched a bit more TV with her sister and chatted happily with her family over tea.

Finally, the happy girl got to the end of her day. She brushed her teeth again, neatly folded her clothes up and said goodnight to her sister, mum and dad. What a lovely day she had had! She was very grateful for everything, and before she fell asleep she said a little prayer. 'Thank you, God, for all the good things I have—my lovely family, my home, food to eat, friends to play with and even going to school. Thank you for today. Amen.'

Then she fell asleep, dreaming of all the other good things that were going to happen.

Now ask the children, 'What was the difference between the miserable boy and the happy girl?'

Reproduced with permission from *Collective Worship for Primary Schools* by Helen Jaeger (Barnabas in Schools, 2016) www.barnabasinschools.org.uk

- Did they do the same things?
- Did they eat the same food?
- Did they have the same kind of family?
- Did they both go to school?
- Did they both have friends?

Yes—so what made the difference? Of course, the answer is: their attitude. The miserable boy was miserable because he always looked at things from a bad point of view and never said 'thank you'. The happy girl was happy because she looked at things from a good point of view and always said 'thank you'.

Thought for the day

Our attitudes can make us happy or miserable. Being thankful often makes us feel much happier.

What the Bible says

Saying thank you to Jesus

Now on his way to Jerusalem, Jesus travelled along the border between Samaria and Galilee. As he was going into a village, ten men who had leprosy met him. They stood at a distance and called out in a loud voice, 'Jesus, Master, have pity on us!' When he saw them, he said, 'Go, show yourselves to the priests.' And as they went, they were cleansed.

One of them, when he saw he was healed, came back, praising God in a loud voice. He threw himself at Jesus' feet and thanked him—and he was a Samaritan. Jesus asked, 'Were not all ten cleansed? Where are the other nine? Has no one returned to give praise to God except this foreigner?' Then he said to him, 'Rise and go; your faith has made you well.'

LUKE 17:11–19

Questions

- How many lepers did Jesus heal?
- How many lepers said 'thank you' to Jesus?
- How do you think Jesus would have felt about this?
- Do you think it made the leper happy to say 'thank you'?

Reflection

Ask the children to close their eyes and think quietly about what they've heard today.

Prayer

Thank you, Jesus, for all the good things you give to us. There are so many that we can hardly even count them. Just like the happy girl in the story, we have so many things to be grateful for. Help us always to appreciate what we have, to say 'thank you' and to be grateful. Amen

13 Caring for each other

Before you start

Buy a tin of stew, but replace the label with one from a tin of cat or dog food.

Opener: What does the label tell us?

Show the tin clearly to the children. Read out what it says on the label and ask who would like to eat that food. Explain that you're really hungry and you forgot to have breakfast today. Casually open the tin, take a fork and begin to eat from it. Make sure you make happy eating noises as you do so, and enjoy the children's reaction.

Next, ask if anyone else would like to try some. (You may have a few volunteers, and it's up to you whether you let them eat it or not.)

Now explain to the children that they all thought you were eating dog food, but in fact you'd changed the label on the tin before you started. In fact, the tin contained normal stew, which was fine to eat. They were judging what you were eating on appearance only. Caring about other people means that we don't judge them, especially on appearances only.

Thought for the day

Explain that we all make up ideas of what people are like, based simply on their appearance or on a tiny bit that we know about them—perhaps something we've heard from other people. But that may not be the truth about what's on the inside of the person. It's only by getting to know people that we find out what they're really like. We care for others by getting to know them properly.

What the Bible says

Why it's important not to judge people

My brothers and sisters, believers in our glorious Lord Jesus Christ must not show favouritism. Suppose a man comes into your meeting wearing a gold ring and fine clothes, and a poor man in filthy old clothes also comes in. If you show special attention to the man wearing fine clothes and say, 'Here's a good seat for you,' but say to the poor man, 'You stand there' or 'Sit on the floor by my feet,' have you not discriminated among yourselves and become judges with evil thoughts? Listen, my dear brothers and sisters: has not God chosen those who are poor in the eyes of the world to be rich in faith and to inherit the kingdom he promised those who love him?

JAMES 2:1–5

Questions

- What is 'favouritism'? (It's when we treat one person better than someone else.)
- How can we show that we care about people?
- How can we include everyone?

Reflection

Ask the children to close their eyes and think quietly about what they've heard today.

Invite them to think about someone they avoid because of the way they look or speak or act. Invite them to include that person in their lessons or in their games at break time today.

Prayer

Thank you, Jesus, that you don't judge people by what they look like or how they act or speak. You look at what they are like on the inside. Help us to do the same and not to judge other people. Amen

14 Celebrating

Before you start

Bring to assembly some materials for a party. They could include paper plates and cups, a colourful tablecloth, party hats and music. You will also need some party food in bowls, such as popcorn, cut-up fruit and vegetables, crisps, sausage rolls and biscuits. Lay out your party table at the front of assembly before it starts.

Opener: Come to my party

Explain that you've decided to throw a surprise party and you'd like to invite eight children to come to it. Now choose your children. You could do this randomly or choose them based on:

- different classes
- birthdays
- teacher nominations
- pupil nominations
- letters of the alphabet
- quiz questions to be answered correctly

Invite the eight children forward, get them seated and serve them some food while they enjoy listening to the party music and wearing their party hats.

Now ask all the children, 'Who has recently been to a party? Why was there a party and who was it for? What did you wear? What did you eat? Did you play any games? What is it like going to a party?'

Allow the eight children at the front to finish a few of their party snacks, and then tell them that the party is over for now. Encourage all the children to try to include others when they have a party.

Thought for the day

We all like going to parties to have fun, spend time with friends and family, eat tasty food and play some games. We all like to be included in fun things.

What the Bible says

Jesus calls a party at someone's house

Jesus entered Jericho and was passing through. A man was there by the name of Zacchaeus; he was a chief tax collector and was wealthy. He wanted to see who Jesus was, but because he was short he could not see over the crowd. So he ran ahead and climbed a sycamore-fig tree to see him, since Jesus was coming that way.

When Jesus reached the spot, he looked up and said to him, 'Zacchaeus, come down immediately. I must stay at your house today.' So he came down at once and welcomed him gladly.

All the people saw this and began to mutter, 'He has gone to be the guest of a sinner.'

But Zacchaeus stood up and said to the Lord, 'Look, Lord! Here and now I give half of my possessions to the poor, and if I have cheated anybody out of anything, I will pay back four times the amount.'

LUKE 19:1–8

Questions

Explain that tax collectors were not very popular people in Jesus' day. They were often rich and took more money than they should.

- Where was Zacchaeus when Jesus spotted him?
- Where did they go for the party, and what did everyone else think about it?
- What effect did the party have on Zacchaeus?

Reflection

Ask the children to close their eyes and think quietly about what they've heard today.

Prayer

Thank you, Jesus, that you loved going to parties and celebrating. We love having fun too. Help us to celebrate well and to include everyone in our celebrations, especially people who might otherwise feel left out. Amen

15 Copying good behaviour

Before you start

No special preparation is required.

Opener: Do this/do that

Play a game of 'Do this/do that'. You can either ask for some volunteers to come to the front or you can play it as a whole assembly, staff included.

Explain that you are going to do an action—for example, touch your nose, raise your hand or hop on one foot. If you say, 'Do this', everyone should copy what you are doing, but if you say, 'Do that', everyone should ignore what you are doing.

Play several rounds.

Thought for the day

Explain that it's easy to copy what other people do, even when you know you shouldn't be doing it. Sometimes we even get into habits of good and bad behaviour. It's important to think about our actions. All it takes is a little thought.

What the Bible says

Jesus asks his followers to do the right thing

Then Jesus said to the crowds and to his disciples: 'The teachers of the law and the Pharisees sit in Moses' seat. So you must be careful to do everything they tell you. But do not do what they do, for they do not practise what they preach. They tie up heavy, cumbersome loads and put them on other people's shoulders, but they themselves are not willing to lift a finger to move them.'

MATTHEW 23:1–4

Explain that the teachers of the law and the Pharisees were the leaders in Jesus' time and people looked to them for advice on how to live.

Questions

- According to Jesus, did the teachers of the law and the Pharisees do what they told others to do or not?
- Did Jesus say that the people should copy their behaviour or not? Why?
- What would be good things for us to copy?

Reflection

Ask the children to close their eyes and think quietly about what they've heard today.

Prayer

Thank you, Jesus, that you always set a good example. When you told other people to do something, like loving each other, you did it yourself. Help us to live well, so that we set a good example to everyone around us as well. Amen

16 Falling out and making up

Before you start

Prepare a list of suggested argument scenarios—for example, arguments over:

- a football game
- food
- use of the TV remote or computer
- a brother or sister taking something that does not belong to them
- name calling

Opener: The argument

Find two children who can act or would enjoy acting, and invite them to the front. Ask them to act out an argument. They can choose their own scenario, or they can take something from your list of suggestions.

Freeze the action at the point where the argument is most heated.

Now ask the rest of the children how they think the argument could be resolved. Will one person say sorry? Will one person back down? Who is in the right and who is in the wrong, or are both people naughty for arguing?

Invite the actors to finish the argument in two ways—one where they don't resolve the problem and one where they do resolve it, perhaps using the ideas that have been shared.

You could repeat the game with a second pair of actors and a different scenario.

Ask the children to think of a time when they had an argument. What was it about? Who did it involve? How did it get resolved?

Thought for the day

Even very good friends can fall out or have a misunderstanding. The important thing is to make up quickly and to say 'sorry' if you've done something wrong. That way, the problem can be solved.

What the Bible says

Joseph forgives his brothers

Tell the children that Joseph had lots of brothers, and they did a very bad thing: they tried to kill him. He was rescued but was taken away by slave traders to live in another country. Eventually he was reunited with his bad brothers, who decided to say 'sorry'.

Joseph's brothers… sent this message to Joseph: 'Before your father died, he instructed us to say to you: "Please forgive your brothers for the great wrong they did to you—for their sin in treating you so cruelly." So we, the servants of the God of your father, beg you to forgive our sin.' When Joseph received the message, he broke down and wept. Then his brothers came and threw themselves down before Joseph. 'Look, we are your slaves!' they said.

GENESIS 50:15–18 (NLT)

Questions

- In this story, Joseph's brothers had done something very wrong. What did they do to put it right?
- What effect did it have on Joseph when they said sorry?
- Do you think they became friends again afterwards?

Reflection

Ask the children to close their eyes and think quietly about what they've heard today.

Prayer

Thank you, Jesus, that even if we argue with someone or make a mistake, we can still say sorry. Help us to be quick to say sorry if we do or say something wrong. If someone does or says something wrong to us, help us to forgive them, as you forgive everyone who says sorry to you. Amen

17 Family

Before you start

Prepare a visual display to illustrate the groups of animals in the list below.

Opener: Animal quiz

Explain that English is a funny language, because we have special names for groups of things—like a 'pad' of paper or a 'box' of crayons. We even have special names for groups of animals. Ask the children if they know what animals are described by each of the following group names.

- Colony (ants)
- Gaggle (geese)
- Parliament (owls)
- Squabble (seagulls)
- Kindle (kittens)
- School (fish)
- Litter (puppies)

Ask the children to come up with a group name for children—for example, a 'chattering' of children.

Explain that the names we give to groups of things are a bit like family names.

Families come in all shapes and sizes. Some people live with their mum or dad or both. You may have a grandma or grandad who looks after you, you may have been adopted, or you may live with a foster family or in a children's home. When you're at school, that's a kind of family, too, where people look out for each other and care for each other.

Say that whoever you live with, God designed it so that you'd have people around you to look after you and love you.

Thought for the day

Christians believe that God made us to live together, and we live in families, groups and communities. Although we are unique and special, we are also part of groups where we look after each other.

What the Bible says

A dad asks Jesus to help his daughter

A synagogue leader came and knelt before [Jesus] and said, 'My daughter has just died. But come and put your hand on her, and she will live.' Jesus got up and went with him, and so did his disciples…

When Jesus entered the synagogue leader's house and saw the noisy crowd and the people playing pipes, he said, 'Go away. The girl is not dead but asleep.' But they laughed at him. After the crowd had been put outside, he went in and took the girl by the hand, and she got up. News of this spread through all that region.

MATTHEW 9:18–19, 23–26

Questions

- What did the synagogue leader ask Jesus to do?
- How do you think the synagogue leader felt when he asked Jesus to help? How did he feel after the miracle had happened?
- How can we show our families we love them?

Reflection

Ask the children to close their eyes and think quietly about what they've heard today.

Prayer

Thank you, Jesus, for our families, our school, our sports teams and our friends. It's good to be together with other people. Help us today, especially, to look out for anyone who isn't part of a group and invite them into ours. Amen

18 Follow the star

Before you start

Cut out ten large stars from coloured paper or card and lay them on the floor or stage at the front of the assembly hall. On each star, write a word—for example, happy, kind, friendly, giving, thoughtful, sharing, funny, honest, polite and caring. If you wish, gather a range of images of people using stars for navigation.

Opener: You're a star

Invite ten children to the front and ask them to choose the star they like best. Ask them to stand facing the other children in the hall, holding their star so that no one else can see the word written on it.

As they stand in the line, ask them to reveal the words on their stars. Ask each child why they chose the star they did.

Thought for the day

Happiness, friendliness, being giving or being thoughtful are all good qualities that make us and the people around us feel better. Sometimes we even call someone a 'star' if they do something good, kind or helpful.

Such qualities are a bit like the stars in the sense that they can guide us on our way in life. People in olden times used the position of the stars to navigate around the world, and people at sea often still do this to map out their journey. (You could show your images of people using stars to navigate.)

What the Bible says

The wise men follow a star

Remind the children of the story of the wise men who followed a star. Ask them to imagine being one of the wise men following the star on a journey. How would they have felt? What would they have seen? Where would they have been?

After Jesus was born in Bethlehem in Judea, during the time of King Herod, Magi from the east came to Jerusalem and asked, 'Where is the one who has been born king of the Jews? We saw his star when it rose and have come to worship him.'

When King Herod heard this he was disturbed, and all Jerusalem with him…

Then Herod called the Magi secretly and found out from them the exact time the star had appeared. He sent them to Bethlehem and said, 'Go and search carefully for the child. As soon as you find him, report to me, so that I too may go and worship him.'

After they had heard the king, they went on their way, and the star they had seen when it rose went ahead of them until it stopped over the place where the child was. When they saw the star, they were overjoyed. On coming to the house, they saw the child with his mother Mary, and they bowed down and worshipped him. Then they opened their treasures and presented him with gifts of gold, frankincense and myrrh. And having been warned in a dream not to go back to Herod, they returned to their country by another route.

MATTHEW 2:1–3, 7–12

Questions

- How did the star help the wise men (or Magi) to find their way?
- What did they find at the end of their starlit journey?
- What does it feel like when you find something that you've been looking for? How do you think the wise men might have felt?

Reflection

Ask the children to close their eyes and think quietly about what they've heard today.

Prayer

Thank you, Jesus, that you are like a big guiding star in our lives. Thank you that you show us the way to go. Thank you that you light up our paths. Amen

19 Gifts and talents

Before you start

If you wish, prepare a slideshow to illustrate the contests listed below.

Opener: Talent competitions

Ask the children to put their hand up if they've got a special talent. Invite individual children to the front to show what they can do—for example, dance, sing, tell jokes, run on the spot, do press-ups or pull funny faces. Then ask if they've ever heard of the following:

- Air Guitar Championships
- Extreme Ironing World Championships
- World's Ugliest Dog Contest
- World Beard and Moustache Championships
- World Black Pudding Throwing Contest
- World Conker Championships
- Worm Charming Championships

They are all real talent competitions from around the world. (Illustrate with a slideshow, if you wish.)

Thought for the day

We all have different talents—special gifts that have been given to us. Some of us are really sporty, some of us are creative, some of us are good at reading and some of us are good at maths. There will be lots of talents represented in the room. Encourage the children to have a go at using their talents today.

What the Bible says

Jesus talks about using our gifts

Jesus told a story about a man going on a journey, who gave money to his servants. Here's what happened.

To one he gave five bags of gold, to another two bags, and to another one bag, each according to his ability. Then he went on his journey. The man who had received five bags of gold went at once and put his money to work and gained five bags more. So also, the one with two bags of gold gained two more. But the man who had received one bag went off, dug a hole in the ground and hid his master's money.

After a long time the master of those servants returned and settled accounts with them. The man who had received five bags of gold brought the other five. 'Master,' he said, 'you entrusted me with five bags of gold. See, I have gained five more.'

His master replied, 'Well done, good and faithful servant! You have been faithful with a few things; I will put you in charge of many things. Come and share your master's happiness!'

The man with two bags of gold also came. 'Master,' he said, 'you entrusted me with two bags of gold: see, I have gained two more.'

His master replied, 'Well done, good and faithful servant! You have been faithful with a few things; I will put you in charge of many things. Come and share your master's happiness!'

Then the man who had received one bag of gold came. 'Master,' he said, 'I knew that you are a hard man, harvesting where you have not sown and gathering where you have not scattered seed. So I was afraid and went out and hid your gold in the ground. See, here is what belongs to you.'

His master replied, 'You wicked, lazy servant! So you knew that I harvest where I have not sown and gather where I have not scattered seed? Well then, you should have put my money on deposit with the bankers, so that when I returned I would have received it back with interest.'

MATTHEW 25:15–27

Questions

- What did each servant do?
- What did the master say to the lazy servant?
- If the money represents gifts from God to people, what does the story say about using our gifts?

Reflection

Ask the children to close their eyes and think quietly about what they've heard today.

Prayer

Thank you, Jesus, that you give us all different gifts and abilities. Thank you that we can share those gifts with each other. Thank you that you made us all talented. Amen

20 Going on holiday

Before you start

Bring to assembly a suitcase packed with some holiday items—for example, sunscreen lotion, swimsuit, bucket, spade, book, hat, towel, map, sunglasses and music player.

Opener: What do you take on holiday?

Carry the suitcase to the front of the assembly, making a big show of it. You could pretend it's very heavy and ask some children to help you carry it, or puff and groan as you move it. Once at the front of the assembly, you could again make a big deal of getting the suitcase on to a stage or chair.

Explain to the children that, as soon as assembly finishes, you're going on holiday, and that's why you've brought your suitcase with you. Ask them if they've ever been on holiday. What kind of places have they been to?

Now ask them to help you check that you've got everything you need. Fiddle with the lock on the suitcase before flinging it open. Bring out the items one at a time and ask the children if you need each one. When you've finished unpacking the suitcase, ask them if there's anything you've forgotten. You could write up their ideas on a board or a large piece of paper. You can make the list as humorous as you like.

When the children have finished contributing, read out everything they've said to you and comment on it. Then look puzzled. Ask the children if there's something else you could take on holiday—maybe not something you'd put in your suitcase, but definitely something that would help you to have a good time. Give the children a chance to come up with some ideas.

Finally, explain that, as well as taking essential things like swimsuits and sunglasses when we go on holiday, it's good to take with us other things—things that are inside us, such as a kind attitude to the people we're travelling with, who might be our brothers and sisters. It's also good to take with us patience, because it can take a long time to get to where we're going; or enthusiasm, so that we really enjoy the holiday.

Thought for the day

As well as the physical things, taking a positive attitude on holiday is important, not just for ourselves but for the other people around us. That way, we can have the best holiday ever.

What the Bible says

Jesus takes his friends on holiday

Then, because so many people were coming and going that they did not even have a chance to eat, [Jesus] said to [his disciples], 'Come with me by yourselves to a quiet place and get some rest.'

MARK 6:31

Questions

- What did Jesus say to his friends?
- Why did he say it to them?
- Do you find it easy or difficult to rest? Why?

Reflection

Ask the children to close their eyes and think quietly about what they've heard today.

Prayer

Thank you, Jesus, for the gift of holidays. We love to go away or to spend time at home with our friends and family. Keep us safe as we travel and help us to enjoy the time we have on holiday. Amen

21 Good choices

Before you start

No special preparation is required.

Opener: Choose carefully

Ask for ten volunteers and line them up, one behind another, all facing in the same direction. Explain that they are going to be allowed to turn and face the person behind them and do one action to them. For example, they could touch their arm, hug them, ruffle their hair, pull their tie (gently), pinch them, stand on their foot, nudge them, wink at them, smile at them or tickle them.

Give the volunteers a few moments to decide what they're going to do. Tell them that once they've decided, they are not allowed to change their mind.

Now explain that whatever they do to the person behind them, that person is allowed to do the same thing back to them. Have they changed their mind? Too late! Play the game.

Explain that although we might think it's fun to do something naughty or not very kind to someone else, we usually don't find it fun when it's done to us.

Thought for the day

The best thing to do is to treat other people as we would like to be treated. Encourage the children to be nice to the people around them today.

What the Bible says

Explain that Jesus encouraged people to make good choices and to help others.

On another Sabbath he went into the synagogue and was teaching, and a man was there whose right hand was shrivelled. The Pharisees and the teachers of the law were looking for a reason to accuse Jesus, so they watched him closely to see if he would heal on the Sabbath. But Jesus knew what they were thinking and said to the man with the shrivelled hand, 'Get up and stand in front of everyone.' So he got up and stood there.

Then Jesus said to them, 'I ask you, which is lawful on the Sabbath: to do good or to do evil, to save life or to destroy it?'

He looked round at them all, and then said to the man, 'Stretch out your hand.' He did so, and his hand was completely restored.

LUKE 6:6–10

Questions

- What problem did the man in this reading have?
- Which was more important to the Pharisees—to be kind or to follow the law? Why do you think they felt like this?
- How do you think the man with the shrivelled hand felt before Jesus healed him and afterwards?

Reflection

Ask the children to close their eyes and think quietly about what they've heard today.

Prayer

Thank you, Jesus, that you gave us the ability to know what is good to do and what is bad to do. Help us to make good choices today in the way that we behave. Help us always to be kind and generous to the people around us. Amen

22 Growing and learning

Before you start

Prepare a game that you can play, either online and with a projector or large enough for everyone in assembly to see it (for example, a game like Hangman).

Opener: Can you work it out?

Invite a child to the front to lead a game of Hangman. Ask the other children to suggest a category—for example, food, sea life, animals or colours—from which the leading child can choose a word. Take suggestions of letters and, after each one, ask if anyone knows the answer.

As soon as a child has the correct answer, he or she can swap with the one at the front. Play several rounds.

At the end, say that it's fun to play games. Some games we know and others we don't know. How do we learn to play them? We can read the rules, we can watch other people playing and we can have a go ourselves.

Thought for the day

We may not always know how to do something, but we can have fun trying, learning and growing in our knowledge. It's OK to be a child and to grow and learn.

What the Bible says

Jesus grew up too

And as Jesus grew up, he increased in wisdom and in favour with God and people.

LUKE 2:52 (TNIV)

Questions

- What sorts of things would Jesus have learnt as a child?
- What is wisdom? Can you think of some examples of it in daily life?
- How does it make you feel to know Jesus was once a child, just like you?

Reflection

Ask the children to close their eyes and think quietly about what they've heard today.

Prayer

Thank you, Jesus, that you understand what it's like to be a child, because you were once one, too. You had to learn things, as we do. Help us to grow up in good ways, just like you. Amen

23 Home

Before you start

Create a visual presentation of different animals and the places where they live. You could include the ant (colony), fox (hole), badger (sett), polar bear (snow hole), rabbit (warren), horse (stable), bat (cave), beaver (lodge), bees (hive), dog (kennel), chicken (coop), aardvark (burrow), ape (logging), cat (lair), dove (dovecote), pig (sty), tropical fish (aquarium), other sea life (coral), rook (rookery), eagle (eyrie), other birds (nest).

Opener: Who lives here?

Show your visual presentation and ask the children if they can guess which animal lives where. You could give out prizes for the answers to the most difficult questions.

Next, ask the children to think about their own homes. What do they like about their homes? What makes them special? Who lives there?

Finally, ask the children to imagine what it would be like not to have a home to live in. Explain that some people in the world are sad because they don't have a home like other people. The good news is that, often, charities or kind people help those who are homeless, so that they have somewhere to live and be looked after.

Thought for the day

Home is important to everyone. We can be thankful for our own homes and help people who don't have anywhere to live.

What the Bible says

How lovely is your dwelling place, O Lord of hosts! My soul longs, indeed it faints for the courts of the Lord; my heart and my flesh sing for joy to the living God. Even the sparrow finds a home, and the swallow a nest for herself, where she may lay her young, at your altars, O Lord of hosts, my King and my God. Happy are those who live in your house, ever singing your praise.

PSALM 84:1–4 (NRSV)

Questions

The person who wrote this psalm would have written it as a song.

- Where does the singer say is the best place to be?
- What do the birds in the song do?
- What is your picture of the perfect home?

Reflection

Ask the children to close their eyes and think quietly about what they've heard today.

Prayer

Thank you, Jesus, that you give us homes to live in. Thank you that all our homes are different. Thank you, too, that you look after all the animals, birds, fish and insects, so that they have homes to live in. Help us to take care of our homes and the homes of others, and please help anyone who doesn't have a home today to find one. Amen

24 Keeping going

Before you start

Bring with you four stopwatches and (if you wish) a small trophy, medal or certificate. You might also like to prepare to tell the story of 'The tortoise and the hare'.

Opener: Sporty challenges

Ask the children to nominate four of the most sporty children in the school. (If you wish, try to make sure there is a range of different ages represented.) Now ask for four volunteers who think they know how to use a stopwatch.

Explain that you're going to set the children a range of challenges and see who the winner is. Ask the children with the stopwatches to set them for a minute. Keep count of how well each volunteer does.

For example, you could count:

- the most star jumps in a minute
- the most sit-ups in a minute
- the most squats in a minute
- the most burpees in a minute

Other challenges you could set might include:

- the fastest lap of the hall
- running on the spot for the longest time

The children with the stopwatches can then compare times.

Declare a winner and, if you like, give them the small trophy, medal or certificate.

Now ask the children: what makes someone fit? How do people get good at sport? What important abilities do they need to have?

Explain that one of the most important skills that someone can have—not just for sport but for everything else too—is perseverance. Ask the children if they know what perseverance means, and explain its definition. (If you have time, you could also read or show a clip of the story 'The tortoise and the hare'.)

Invite the children to adopt a persevering attitude in all they do, perhaps by using a phrase like 'I can and I will' or 'Just keep going' for the rest of the day.

Thought for the day

We may not always find it easy to do things, but, if we keep going with a positive attitude, we often find that we can do more than we ever thought we could.

What the Bible says

Running a good race

Explain that Jesus had amazing sticking power. He had to go to the cross to save everybody, which was a very hard thing to do. It would have been easy to give up or not even start, but he kept going, even though he knew he would have to die. He did it because he loved people and wanted to save them. After he had achieved what he set out to do, God raised him from the dead, and now Jesus is alive again in heaven.

Therefore, since we are surrounded by so great a cloud of witnesses, let us also lay aside every weight and the sin that clings so closely, and let us run with perseverance the race that is set before us, looking to Jesus the pioneer and perfecter of our faith, who for the sake of the joy that was set before him endured the cross, disregarding its shame, and has taken his seat at the right hand of the throne of God.

HEBREWS 12:1–2 (NRSV)

Questions

- What is 'endurance' and why do we need it?
- How does it feel when we achieve something that was hard to do?
- Have you ever faced a challenge? What was it?
- What can help us as we try to keep going?

Reflection

Ask the children to close their eyes and think quietly about what they've heard today.

Prayer

Thank you, Jesus, that you help us to keep going, even when things are tough. Thank you that you give us your strength to keep going. Help us to achieve the good things you've given us to do. Amen

25 Knowing all about you

Before you start

Conduct a quick survey of staff in school to find out their answers to the following:

- favourite colour
- favourite animal
- favourite activity
- favourite word
- favourite game
- favourite food
- favourite book
- favourite superhero
- favourite TV programme
- favourite film
- favourite way to relax

Bring the answers to the assembly, with the name of each staff member at the top of their list.

Opener: Who is it?

Explain that we all know lots about each other. Read out the answers to your questions and ask the children to say which staff member they think gave those answers.

Thought for the day

We are all unique people, with special things that we like, do and say. God loves each one of us very much.

What the Bible says

God knows you very well

Jesus wanted people to understand how much God loved them, so he told them this:

'Are not two sparrows sold for a penny? Yet not one of them will fall to the ground outside your Father's care. And even the very hairs of your head are all numbered. So don't be afraid; you are worth more than many sparrows.'

MATTHEW 10:29–31

Questions

- How many hairs do you think you have on your head?
- How long would it take you to count each single one?
- If God knows every single hair on your head, what might that tell you about him?

Reflection

Ask the children to close their eyes and think quietly about what they've heard today.

Prayer

Thank you, Jesus, that you love all of us and know everything about each one of us, even down to how many single strands of hair we have on our heads. Thank you for your love. Amen

26 Laughing is good for you

Before you start

Bring to assembly a joke book with some good jokes marked in it.

Opener: Tell me a joke

Ask the children to tell you their favourite jokes. Then ask them to put their hands up if they think the following statements are true. Read out the statements in order. (They are all true.)

- Laughter relaxes your body.
- Laughter keeps you well and helps to stop you getting ill.
- Laughter keeps your heart healthy.
- Laughter makes you feel pain less.
- Laughter helps you to feel happier.
- Laughter is good for friendship.

Ask the children if they think it's important to have fun, and what kinds of things they do to have fun or to make them laugh. Answers might include being with friends, watching something funny on TV, playing a game or going bowling.

Thought for the day

Isn't it amazing that having fun could be so good for you? Christians believe that God made the human body so that we would enjoy having fun and laughing. There's even a saying that 'laughter is the best medicine', because it helps to keep us healthy.

What the Bible says

God enjoys it when we laugh

When the Lord restored the fortunes of Zion, we were like those who dreamed. Our mouths were filled with laughter, our tongues with songs of joy. Then it was said among the nations, 'The Lord has done great things for them.' The Lord has done great things for us and we are filled with joy.

PSALM 126:1–3

Questions

- How do we feel when we enjoy something?
- Who can make us happy, and how, according to this psalm?
- How might God feel when we laugh?

Reflection

Ask the children to close their eyes and think quietly about what they've heard today.

Prayer

Thank you, Jesus, for the gifts of laughter and fun. All of us like to have fun sometimes. Thank you that you even made laughter good for us. Help us to have fun today—fun that includes everyone and is never hurtful. Amen

27 Learning from each other

Before you start

No special preparation is required.

Opener: Learn a new language

Ask the children to put up their hands if their main language is not English. Invite several of those children to the front. (Try to ensure that, between them, they speak a range of different languages.)

Ask each volunteer to teach the rest of the school a phrase in their language—for example, 'good morning' or 'hello'. The child can say the phrase, then ask the others in assembly to repeat it with them, before finally saying their phrase and letting the rest of the school repeat it without help.

Now ask each volunteer to tell the rest of the school something about themselves in their own language and to translate it into English. Alternatively, ask them a series of questions and let them respond in their own language, followed by a translation.

You could ask questions such as:

- Where do you live?
- How old are you?
- What is your name?
- Who is your best friend?
- What is your favourite subject at school?
- Do you have any brothers or sisters and, if so, what are their names?
- What is your favourite food?
- Do you have any pets?
- What activities do you like to do at the weekend?

When you have finished, thank your volunteers and ask them to sit down.

Ask the children if they've ever visited a country where English was not the main language. Was it easy or hard to understand what people were saying? What was it like, travelling around or buying food?

Explain that it's fun to learn different languages.

Thought for the day

It's amazing that God created so many people around the world, speaking so many different languages. It can be fun to learn from each other.

What the Bible says

Many people, many languages

Note: you may prefer to read out this passage yourself, rather than asking a child to do it, as there are some especially difficult words to pronounce.

Suddenly a sound like the blowing of a violent wind came from heaven and filled the whole house where they were sitting. They saw what seemed to be tongues of fire that separated and came to rest on each of them. All of them were filled with the Holy Spirit and began to speak in other tongues as the Spirit enabled them.

Now there were staying in Jerusalem God-fearing Jews from every nation under heaven. When they heard this sound, a crowd came together in bewilderment, because each one heard their own language being spoken. Utterly amazed, they asked: 'Aren't all these who are speaking Galileans? Then how is it that each of us hears them in our native language? Parthians, Medes and Elamites; residents of Mesopotamia, Judea and Cappadocia, Pontus and Asia, Phrygia and Pamphylia, Egypt and the parts of Libya near Cyrene; visitors from Rome (both Jews and converts to Judaism); Cretans and Arabs—we hear them declaring the wonders of God in our own tongues!'

ACTS 2:1–11

Questions

- Can you name any of the languages that would have been spoken by the people that day?
- Do you know, or can you guess, how many nationalities are mentioned in the reading? (15)

Reflection

Ask the children to close their eyes and think quietly about what they've heard today.

Prayer

Thank you, Jesus, that there are so many amazing countries and languages around the world. Help us to learn from each other's customs and cultures. Amen

28 Looking forward

Before you start

If you wish, prepare a montage of images of people celebrating birthdays, Christmas or Easter, or attending other parties.

Opener: Birthdays, Christmas, Easter and celebrations

Ask a whole class to stand up. It could be a class at the front, in the middle or at the back of the assembly hall. Ask the children to think about one thing they are looking forward to this year. Give them a few moments to think.

Then ask them to sit down (in sequence) if they thought of:

1. Birthday
2. Christmas
3. Easter
4. Family party

These events should cover most of the class, but if there are a few children still standing, invite them to tell everyone what they are looking forward to the most. When all the children have answered, make sure everyone is sitting down.

Ask why it is that we look forward to birthdays, Christmas, Easter or family parties. You'll probably have a range of answers, from getting presents to eating yummy food or wearing party clothes. A few might say they like to be with their family or to see people happy.

You could now show your images of people celebrating. As you look through the images, agree that we all enjoy such events because they make us feel happy, special and loved.

Thought for the day

Looking forward to things is an important part of life. We all like to anticipate fun or exciting things that are going to happen in the future.

What the Bible says

The wise men follow a star

Remind the children of the story of the wise men who followed a star. Ask them, as you read the story, to think about what the wise men would have been looking forward to. What did they expect to see? Who did they expect to meet? What would it have felt like to see the baby Jesus, who they believed to be a special king?

After they had heard the king, [the wise men] went on their way, and the star they had seen when it rose went ahead of them until it stopped over the place where the child was. When they saw the star, they were overjoyed. On coming to the house, they saw the child with his mother Mary, and they bowed down and worshipped him. Then they opened their treasures and presented him with gifts of gold, frankincense and myrrh. And having been warned in a dream not to go back to Herod, they returned to their country by another route.

MATTHEW 2:9–12

Questions

- In this reading, which word tells us exactly how the wise men felt when they saw the star?
- What did they do when they met Jesus?
- What kind of present would you have brought to the baby Jesus?
- How do you think the wise men would have felt as they journeyed back home?

Reflection

Ask the children to close their eyes and think quietly about what they've heard today.

Prayer

Thank you, Jesus, that you give us good things to look forward to. Thank you that you think celebrating is important. Please give us lots of joy and happiness. Amen

29 Making mistakes

Before you start

Prearrange a volunteer to bring you the following items as you read the story below: a cuddly toy dog, a diary, a cup of coffee and a piece of paper.

Opener: Owning up

Read out the following story.

(Apologetically) I've got something to tell you. I know it's meant to be assembly today, but unfortunately I'm not going to be able to do it.

You see, my dog ate the piece of paper I wrote everything down on, and then he ran away… *(Volunteer brings the cuddly toy dog.)*

OK, so the thing is, I thought the assembly was going to be on a different day, and… *(Volunteer brings the diary, open at today's date, and points at the word ASSEMBLY underlined in red.)*

Umm, I guess I should come clean. I overslept and didn't have time to drink my coffee this morning. You see, coffee helps me to stay awake, which means I would have remembered to bring the paper that I wrote the assembly down on, so… *(Volunteer brings a cup of half-drunk coffee, along with a piece of paper.)*

OK, no more excuses! I just forgot. Sorry!

Thought for the day

Sometimes, when we make mistakes, we try to cover them up. But it can take a lot more work than just to be honest, tell the truth and say sorry.

What the Bible says

The son who decided to say sorry

If you are not reading this Bible passage yourself, perhaps ask for several children to read parts of it, as it's a long story. Explain that Jesus told a story about a man and his two sons.

There was a man who had two sons. The younger one said to his father, 'Father, give me my share of the estate.' So he divided his property between them.

Not long after that, the younger son got together all he had, set off for a distant country and there squandered his wealth in wild living. After he had spent everything, there was a severe famine in that whole country, and he began to be in need. So he went off and hired himself out to a citizen of that country, who sent him to his field to feed pigs. He longed to fill his stomach with the pods that the pigs were eating, but no one gave him anything.

When he came to his senses, he said, 'How many of my father's hired servants have food to spare, and here I am starving to death! I will set out and go back to my father and say to him: Father, I have sinned against heaven and against you. I am no longer worthy to be called your son; make me like one of your hired servants.' So he got up and went to his father.

But while he was still a long way off, his father saw him and was filled with compassion for him; he ran to his son, threw his arms around him and kissed him. The son said to him, 'Father, I have sinned against heaven and against you. I am no longer worthy to be called your son.'

But the father said to his servants, 'Quick, bring the best robe and put it on him. Put a ring on his finger and sandals on his feet. Bring the fattened calf and kill it. Let's have a feast and celebrate. For this son of mine was dead and is alive again. He was lost and is found.' So they began to celebrate.

LUKE 15:11–24

Questions

Before asking the questions, make sure the children understand any difficult words in the Bible passage.

- What did the younger son do wrong?
- What did he do right?
- If you were his father, would you forgive him?

Reflection

Ask the children to close their eyes and think quietly about what they've heard today.

Prayer

Thank you, Jesus, that you love us as the father in the story loved his son, even when we make mistakes. Thank you that we can say sorry and know you will forgive us. Amen

30 Meeting angels

Before you start

Bring to assembly a large piece of paper and marker pens, and eight smaller pieces of paper.

Opener: Ninja angels

Ask the children if they've ever done something nice for someone. What was it? Maybe it was tidying up, sharing, helping a friend with a problem they were stuck on, playing a game with someone new or lending a classmate something they needed. You could write a few ideas up on a big piece of paper for everyone to see. Make sure that, by the end of your discussion, you have at least eight different ideas.

Invite eight volunteers to come forward from the top year group in the school. Ask each one to write their name on a small piece of paper, fold it up and give it to you.

Explain that we often use the word 'angel' or say 'You're an angel' when someone does something good for us. Tell the children that you'd like your volunteers to be 'angels' for the day, doing something good for someone else. But there's a catch! They must do their good deed without the other person being aware that they're doing it, like a ninja.

Randomly hand out a named piece of paper to each of the volunteers, asking them to keep the names private. Tell them that they need to choose one of the good deeds from the list you made together, and, at some stage during the day, do that good deed for the person whose name they've been given, without the person knowing who has done it. They can only reveal their identity at the end of the day.

When you have set the challenge, let the volunteers return to their seats.

You could invite other year groups to do the same when they get back to class after assembly.

Thought for the day

It's good to do nice things for people, and it can be even more fun to do it without letting the other person know about it. Angels are believed to be messengers from God, who come to give good news or do good things for the people God sends them to.

What the Bible says

Angels bring great news

There were shepherds living out in the fields nearby, keeping watch over their flocks at night. An angel of the Lord appeared to them, and the glory of the Lord shone around them, and they were terrified. But the angel said to them, 'Do not be afraid. I bring you good news that will cause great joy for all the people. Today in the town of David a Saviour has been born to you; he is the Messiah, the Lord. This will be a sign to you: you will find a baby wrapped in cloths and lying in a manger.'

Suddenly a great company of the heavenly host appeared with the angel, praising God and saying, 'Glory to God in the highest heaven and on earth peace to those on whom his favour rests.'

When the angels had left them and gone into heaven, the shepherds said to one another, 'Let's go to Bethlehem and see this thing that has happened, which the Lord has told us about.'

LUKE 2:8–15

Questions

- What news did the angels bring?
- How would you have felt if you had been there?
- What would you have done?

Reflection

Ask the children to close their eyes and think quietly about what they've heard today.

Prayer

Thank you, Jesus, that you have special messengers called angels. Thank you that you send them to guide and help us, bringing us good news and doing good things for us. Please guide and help us today and help us to be 'angels' to other people. Amen

31 More than enough

Before you start

Hide some small packets of sweets around the assembly hall. You could hide them in all sorts of places—under chairs, on shelves, behind gym equipment, or near doors or windows. Also bring a box containing a stash of lots more packets of sweets.

Opener: Can you find the treasure?

Invite three volunteers to the front. Explain that you've hidden several packets of sweets around the room, and it's their job to go on a treasure hunt. Tell them that they will have just a minute to find all the packets of sweets that they can, and they mustn't trip or hurt anyone as they race around the room.

Time the volunteers for a minute before calling them back to the front of the hall. Make a show of counting up the packets of sweets, and declare a winner.

Now tell the volunteers that you have an extra, secret stash of sweets. Ask them if they'd like even more to add to their collection. (They are all likely to say 'yes'.) Open your box and pile extra sweet packets into their arms, until they can't carry any more. (Ensure that the sweets are shared out fairly afterwards.)

Ask: what is it like to be given even more than you thought you could have?

Thought for the day

If we ask for something from God, perhaps we think that we might get just enough, but God is very generous and gives us even more than we need.

What the Bible says

Jesus feeds a huge crowd of people

As evening approached, the disciples came to [Jesus] and said, 'This is a remote place, and it's already getting late. Send the crowds away, so that they can go to the villages and buy themselves some food.'

Jesus replied, 'They do not need to go away. You give them something to eat.'

'We have here only five loaves of bread and two fish,' they answered.

'Bring them here to me,' he said. And he told the people to sit down on the grass. Taking the five loaves and the two fish and looking up to heaven, he gave thanks and broke the loaves. Then he gave them to the disciples, and the disciples gave them to the people. They all ate and were satisfied, and the disciples picked up twelve basketfuls of broken pieces that were left over. The number of those who ate was about five thousand men, besides women and children.

MATTHEW 14:15–21

Questions

- What food did Jesus have to start with?
- What did he do with it?
- How much food was left over?
- How would you have felt if you had been among the crowd?
- What would you have thought and talked about on the way home?

Reflection

Ask the children to close their eyes and think quietly about what they've heard today.

Prayer

Thank you, Jesus, that you are so generous. Sometimes you give us even more than we need. You are very kind. Please help all the people in the world who need something today, and help us to be generous with what we have too. Amen

32 Mother's Day: mums and carers

Before you start

From coloured card, cut out the parts of a large flower: seven big petals, a circle, a stem and two leaves.

Opener: Make a special flower

Ask the children to think of someone who cares for them—a mum, dad, grandparent, other family member, friend or teacher. Write these words in the cardboard circle. Ask two children to come and hold the circle, which will be the centre of your flower. Attach the stem to the flower centre.

Ask the children for ideas of what these people do to show that they care and to make them special. Answers might include: they give me hugs; they listen to me; they play games with me; they make nice food for me to eat; they buy presents for me; they look after me when I'm ill; they read to me; they help me get dressed; they take me to nice places; they let me have sleepovers.

Write the ideas on the cardboard petals. Then ask volunteers to come and stick the petals to the flower centre.

Ask the children for ideas of what they could do to show their appreciation to the people who care for them today. Answers might include: hug them back; do what they say; say thank you; buy them presents.

Write these ideas on the cardboard leaves. Then ask volunteers to come and stick the leaves to the flower stem.

Finally, ask the children what they could say to the people who care for them. Answers might include: thank you; I love you; I'm grateful for what you do for me.

Write these answers on the stem of the flower, and thank the volunteers for their help.

Thought for the day

There are many different kinds of people who care for us, and we may care for people like our family members too. It's good to show our appreciation, and one way to do that is to say 'thank you' or give a gift, like a flower. Remember to say 'thank you' today.

What the Bible says

Jesus asks his friends to care for each other

'A new command I give you: love one another. As I have loved you, so you must love one another. By this everyone will know that you are my disciples, if you love one another.'

JOHN 13:34–35

Questions

- Why do you think Jesus said it was important for people to love one another?
- How does it feel when we know someone loves us?
- How can we show our love to other people? What can we do?

Reflection

Ask the children to close their eyes and think quietly about what they've heard today.

Prayer

Thank you, Jesus, that you give us so many good things, including people who care about us and who we care about too. Help us to remember to say 'thank you', particularly to the special people in our lives. Amen

33 Mother's Day: people who help

Before you start

Bring to assembly two full sets of clothes, one for a girl and one for a boy, in large sizes. You could include (for the girl) dress, cardigan, socks and shoes and (for the boy) trousers, jumper, socks and shoes.

Opener: Who helps you?

Invite two pairs of volunteers to the front. Explain that you're going to time them as they get dressed. In each pair, one person will put the clothes on (over their own clothes) and the other can help them. The winner is the one who is first to get all the clothes on, properly and tidily.

Once the game is over, ask the rest of the children to think about all the people who help them throughout the day. Questions could include:

- Who helps you to make breakfast?
- Who helps you to get dressed?
- Who helps you to get to school?
- Who helps to keep the school tidy?
- Who helps you to learn?
- Who helps you to have fun in the playground?
- Who helps you when you don't know what to do?
- Who helps you when you are sad?
- Who helps you if you hurt yourself?
- Who helps you to eat healthily?
- Who helps you to get home?

Thought for the day

Lots of people help us every day. The police help to keep us safe, bus drivers help us to travel where we want to go, people in shops help us to buy things we like or need, people in bin lorries help to keep our parks and streets clean, and doctors help us to get better.

What the Bible says

Jesus tells a story about what's important

'The King will say to those on his right, "Come, you who are blessed by my Father; take your inheritance, the kingdom prepared for you since the creation of the world. For I was hungry and you gave me something to eat, I was thirsty and you gave me something to drink, I was a stranger and you invited me in, I needed clothes and you clothed me, I was ill and you looked after me, I was in prison and you came to visit me."

'Then the righteous will answer him, "Lord, when did we see you hungry and feed you, or thirsty and give you something to drink? When did we see you a stranger and invite you in, or needing clothes and clothe you? When did we see you ill or in prison and go to visit you?"

The King will reply, "Truly I tell you, whatever you did for one of the least of these brothers and sisters of mine, you did for me."'

MATTHEW 25:34–40

Questions

- In this story, what kind of things did the king reward?
- Were the people who did these things aware that they were doing it for the king?
- What response did the king give to their questions? What did he mean?

Reflection

Ask the children to close their eyes and think quietly about what they've heard today.

Prayer

Thank you, Jesus, for all the people in the world who help each other. Thank you for the people in my life who help me. If someone needs my help today, please help me to give them what they need, quickly and freely. Amen

34 Planting seeds

Before you start

Prepare a slideshow or visual presentation showing different kinds of seeds and the plants that produce them. One of the seeds must be a mustard seed.

Alternatively, bring real seeds to assembly, but make sure all of them (except the mustard seed) are big enough for all the children to see, including those at the back of the hall. You could show an acorn, a melon seed, a pumpkin seed, an avocado seed, a sunflower seed, a cherry seed and an apricot seed. It's best if you find seeds that the children are likely to meet in everyday life.

Opener: What is this and what does it become?

Show each seed and ask the children to say where it comes from. Finally, show the tiny mustard seed and ask if anyone knows what it is.

You could rank the seeds in order of size, from smallest to biggest. Is it surprising to see which seeds produce which fruit or flower?

Thought for the day

Christians believe that God made all the seeds in the world, so that there would always be vegetables, trees and flowers. Isn't it amazing that all these things can grow from seeds?

What the Bible says

A small seed grows into a very big tree

[Jesus] told them another parable: 'The kingdom of heaven is like a mustard seed, which a man took and planted in his field. Though it is the smallest of all seeds, yet when it grows, it is the largest of garden plants and becomes a tree, so that the birds come and perch in its branches.'

MATTHEW 13:31–32

Questions

- According to this story, what seed is God's kingdom like?
- What happens when the mustard tree is fully grown?
- What was Jesus trying to say in this story?
- How was Jesus trying to encourage the people who were listening to him?

Reflection

Ask the children to close their eyes and think quietly about what they've heard today.

Prayer

Thank you, Jesus, for all the trees and plants that grow from seeds, and for the food we grow. We're a bit like those seeds: we are growing too. Please look after us and take care of us as we grow. Amen

35 Prejudice

Before you start

Bring to assembly some pieces of paper and pens, or a box of toys and a bag to hold them all.

You could also download or print off a picture of the story of the good Samaritan, as a visual aid for the Bible story.

Opener: Can you guess?

Invite four or five children to come to the front. Ask them to write on a piece of paper their favourite colour, something they're good at or something they like to do. Hold up each piece of paper, read it out and ask the rest of the children to decide which piece of paper belongs to which of your volunteers. Did they guess right? Why or why not? Is it easy to judge people based on their appearance only?

Alternatively, ask each volunteer to choose a different toy from the box and to keep it hidden from the rest of the children as they put it into a bag. Then pull each toy out of the bag and ask the other children to guess which toy was chosen by each of the volunteers.

Thought for the day

You can't judge what someone is like, just by looking at them. If you judge in this way, it's called 'prejudice', and it's not always caring or kind.

What the Bible says

The true friend

Jesus said: 'A man was going down from Jerusalem to Jericho, when he was attacked by robbers. They stripped him of his clothes, beat him and went away, leaving him half-dead. A priest happened to be going down the same road, and when he saw the man, he passed by on the other side. So, too, a Levite, when he came to the place and saw him, he passed by on the other side. But a Samaritan, as he travelled, came where the man was; and when he saw him, he took pity on him. He went to him and bandaged his wounds, pouring on oil and wine. Then he put the man on his own donkey, brought him to an inn and took care of him. The next day he took out two denarii and gave them to the innkeeper. "Look after him," he said, "and when I return, I will reimburse you for any extra expense you may have."'

LUKE 10:30–35

Questions

Explain that, in Bible times, people judged each other based on appearances, just as we often do today. The Jewish people thought of themselves as being 'in' and people like Samaritans (from a different part of the country) as being 'out'. At the same time, they prided themselves on helping and caring for others.

- In this story, who ignored the injured man?
- Who helped the injured man?
- What point was Jesus trying to make?

Reflection

Ask the children to close their eyes and think quietly about what they've heard today.

Prayer

Thank you, Jesus, that you don't look at outward appearances. What's important to you is our hearts. Help our hearts to be full of good things, like love. Amen

36 Respecting others

Before you start

If you can rehearse the story script with volunteers before assembly, that would be a good idea, but don't worry if not. You can just ask your volunteer actors to make up the actions as they go along.

Opener: A bad manners day

Ask for some volunteers to act out the story as you read it, using simple actions.

There was once a man who had very, very bad manners. He never said 'hello' to anyone, even when they said 'hello' to him. He never smiled at anyone, even when they smiled at him. If someone was walking towards him, he always put his face down and scowled.

One day, Mr Bad Manners went into town. He decided to catch the bus. A woman was trying to get on to the bus with all her shopping. Did he help her? No, he pushed right past her.

There was one seat left at the front of the bus and Mr Bad Manners took it. An old woman came on behind him, carrying a walking stick. Did Mr Bad Manners offer her his seat? No, he did not. Even when another passenger suggested he give up his seat, he wouldn't.

When Mr Bad Manners reached his stop, he barged past the other passengers, without saying 'excuse me' to them or 'thank you' to the driver.

He got off the bus and went into a shop. When he'd found what he wanted, he walked right to the front of the queue. People tutted and sighed, but Mr Bad Manners just ignored them.

The man behind the counter said, 'Excuse me, you can't just push your way to the front of the queue like that!'

But Mr Bad Manners refused to move. Eventually the man had to serve him, just to get rid of him.

Mr Bad Manners then decided to walk home. It started to rain. Mr Bad Manners put up his umbrella. Behind him he heard footsteps. He turned round and saw one of his neighbours, walking a dog. The neighbour was soaked through. Instead of asking the neighbour if he wanted to share his umbrella, Mr Bad Manners just walked faster than ever, scowling in the rain.

Finally, Mr Bad Manners got home. When he'd put away his umbrella, he made himself some tea and toast and sat in front of the fire. 'What a horrible day I've had,' he said to himself. 'Aren't people rude?'

Ask the children: what sort of things did Mr Bad Manners do, that showed he had no manners? What sort of things could he have done, which would have been much more polite?

Thought for the day

It may seem easy to be rude, but it takes quite a lot of effort to have bad manners all the time. Good manners don't cost anything, and they make you and everyone around you feel better.

What the Bible says

Being kind

Be kind to each other, tenderhearted, forgiving one another, just as God through Christ has forgiven you.

EPHESIANS 4:32 (NLT)

Questions

- How does the Bible say we should treat each other?
- How does God treat us?
- How does it make you feel if you treat other people with respect? How do you feel if others respect you?

Reflection

Ask the children to close their eyes and think quietly about what they've heard today.

Prayer

Thank you, Jesus, that you are kind and polite and that you encourage us to be kind and polite to other people. Help us always to show good manners to the people around us. Amen

37 Rest and relaxation

Before you start

Bring to assembly some gentle music to play in the background while you take the children through a relaxation exercise.

Opener: Relax your body and float away

Ask the children to close their eyes. You are going to help them to concentrate on relaxing every part of their body. Ask them to concentrate on:

- their toes, scrunching them up, then relaxing them
- their feet, scrunching them up, then relaxing them
- their calves/bottom of their legs, scrunching them up, then relaxing them
- their thighs/top of their legs, scrunching them up, then relaxing them
- their back, scrunching it up, then relaxing it
- their tummy, scrunching it up, then relaxing it
- their shoulders, scrunching them up, then relaxing them
- their arms, scrunching them up, then relaxing them
- their hands, scrunching them up, then relaxing them
- their fingers, scrunching them up, then relaxing them
- their face, scrunching it up, then relaxing it

Now ask them to imagine they are a fluffy cloud, floating high in the sky on a warm summer's day. They can see everything happening beneath them, but they feel completely calm and relaxed.

Finally, explain that you are going to help them to wake up again. You're going to count to ten and then they can open their eyes again. Count to ten.

Ask the children how they felt when they were relaxing and how they feel now. Do they feel better?

Thought for the day

Christians believe that God made us not only to learn and to work, but to relax too. It's important to relax if we want to be healthy and happy, because that's the way we're made. It feels nice when we relax, especially if we've been working hard.

What the Bible says

Even God rests from work

By the seventh day God had finished the work he had been doing; so on the seventh day he rested from all his work. Then God blessed the seventh day and made it holy, because on it he rested from all the work of creating that he had done.

GENESIS 2:2–3

Questions

- In this reading, what did God do at the end of creating everything?
- Why did God rest?
- Do you think that rest and relaxation are important? If so, why?

Reflection

Ask the children to close their eyes and think quietly about what they've heard today.

Prayer

Thank you, Jesus, that it's good to rest and relax. Thank you that you don't expect us to be learning and working all the time. Even in school we have lunch breaks and play time. Please give us your gift of rest and peace. Amen

38 Role models

Before you start

Prepare a slideshow presentation of some famous inspirational people—for example, Mother Teresa, Martin Luther King, a famous footballer and a famous athlete. Hand out a small slip of paper and pencil to everyone as they come into assembly.

Opener: Drawing on inspiration

Play your slideshow of people who have inspired others throughout history. Ask the children if they know who the people are, why they are famous and why they inspire others. Think about the reasons why people are inspiring. For example, they are honest or courageous or dedicated; they stand up for others, make positive changes happen or make 100 per cent effort.

Ask the children to name one person who inspires them and explain why. They can write the name of the person on their piece of paper, along with one word to say why they are so inspiring.

Now ask the children to turn over their piece of paper and draw a quick picture of themselves. Invite them to write something about themselves that could inspire others—for example, they help others to learn, they are kind, they are fun to be with, they are thoughtful, or they listen and help.

Invite the children to practise their special 'inspirational' qualities throughout the rest of the day.

Thought for the day

Everyone has at least one inspirational quality. It's good to use our special abilities because, that way, we can inspire other people too and encourage them to be and do their best.

What the Bible says

Let your good deeds be seen

'You are the light of the world. A town built on a hill cannot be hidden. Neither do people light a lamp and put it under a bowl. Instead they put it on its stand, and it gives light to everyone in the house. In the same way, let your light shine before others, that they may see your good deeds and glorify your Father in heaven.'

MATTHEW 5:14–16

Questions

- What did Jesus say about where a lamp or light is put?
- Why is it put in that place?
- What did Jesus mean when he said, 'Let your light shine before others'?
- Why might it be good for other people to see our light?

Reflection

Ask the children to close their eyes and think quietly about what they've heard today.

Prayer

Thank you, Jesus, that there are people in the world who have inspired others, perhaps by something they did or said or the way they lived. Help me to inspire other people too, perhaps by behaving well or doing good work today. Amen

39 Saying goodbye

Before you start

Bring to assembly three different sets of clothes, one for the youngest year group present, one for the oldest year group, and one for an adult.

Also, prepare some coloured cards, each with a letter on one side and a word on the other, as below:

- C   constant
- H   happens
- A   amazing
- N   new
- G   good
- E   epic

Opener: Who's ready for change?

Invite to the front a child from the youngest year group in school, one from the oldest year group, and a willing staff member. Hand them each a set of clothes to try on, but make sure they're not the right sizes. Give the volunteers a few moments to get into the clothes you've given them. What do they look like? It should be quite funny. Now invite them to swap clothes with someone else and try again. They should end up with clothes that fit.

Explain that change happens to everyone. One way to see it is in the clothes we wear. The clothes that the oldest children once wore no longer fit them, and the clothes that the youngest children think are much too big will fit them in time. Even the adult clothes will eventually fit them.

Now ask the children how they feel about change. Is it exciting or scary? Is it a good thing or a bad thing? Explain that change can sometimes be any of these things, but having a positive attitude to change can help us to deal with new experiences.

Finally, invite six volunteers to the front and hand them each a coloured card to hold. Ask them to stand with the words facing outwards. As you read each word, they can turn their card over to display the letter. When you've finished reading the words out, the letters will spell the word 'CHANGE'.

Thought for the day

Change happens all the time. It can be scary, but it can also bring exciting new things.

What the Bible says

Jesus invites people to follow him

As Jesus passed along the Sea of Galilee, he saw Simon and his brother Andrew casting a net into the lake—for they were fishermen. And Jesus said to them, 'Follow me and I will make you fish for people.' And immediately they left their nets and followed him. As he went a little farther, he saw James son of Zebedee and his brother John, who were in their boat mending the nets. Immediately he called them; and they left their father Zebedee in the boat with the hired men, and followed him.

MARK 1:16–20 (NRSV)

Questions

- Do you think it would have been hard for Simon and Andrew to leave home and follow Jesus?
- Why do you think they did it?
- What helps us in times of change?

Reflection

Ask the children to close their eyes and think quietly about what they've heard today.

Prayer

Thank you, Jesus, that you are with us all through our lives, from when we are little babies right up to when we get old. Thank you that change can be exciting. Please help us if we get nervous about it. Amen

40 Setting a good example

Before you start

Prepare a simple large spin-wheel, with the circle divided into eight segments of different coloured card. Attach a large arrow spinner, which will spin freely.

Opener: Spin-wheel of good deeds

Invite eight volunteers to the front.

Now ask the rest of the children for eight examples of good behaviour. You could ask for them to be assembly-specific (such as sitting up straight, not fidgeting, not chatting, putting your hand up, carrying the teacher's chair, holding the door open, putting away extra chairs at the end, and filing in or out quietly) or general examples (such as listening to the teacher, not chatting, not fighting, helping others, trying your best, doing what's asked of you, being polite, and sharing well).

As you decide on the examples, write them in large letters on the eight segments of coloured card.

Explain that, sometimes, even though we know what we should do for the best, we don't do it. Sometimes we need help to do it, and one way for us to get help is to watch other people who are behaving well and copy them.

That's just what the eight volunteers are going to do for everyone for the rest of assembly or the whole school day. They're going to show everyone else how well to behave—but they won't have to do everything. They just have to do one thing really, really well.

Now invite your volunteers to spin the arrow. Whichever segment it stops on, that's the action for which they're going to set an exceptional example. Ask each volunteer if they agree. If they do, let them return to their seats and begin to model the good behaviour for everyone else.

Thought for the day

We might not always know the best way to do something, but, by watching other people who are good at it, we can learn. Once we know how to do something really well, we can set a good example for other people, too.

What the Bible says

Jesus describes the kind of people who set a good example

Blessed are the poor in spirit, for theirs is the kingdom of heaven. Blessed are those who mourn, for they will be comforted. Blessed are the meek, for they will inherit the earth. Blessed are those who hunger and thirst for righteousness, for they will be filled. Blessed are the merciful, for they will be shown mercy. Blessed are the pure in heart, for they will see God. Blessed are the peacemakers, for they will be called children of God. Blessed are those who are persecuted because of righteousness, for theirs is the kingdom of heaven.

MATTHEW 5:3–10

Questions

- What kind of people did Jesus say are blessed?
- What kind of example do they set?
- Are you surprised by what Jesus said?
- Did you think Jesus would say that the people who are happy or successful are the ones setting a good example?

Reflection

Ask the children to close their eyes and think quietly about what they've heard today.

Prayer

Thank you, Jesus, that you showed us how to live well, loving ourselves and loving other people around us. Help us to be loving and kind in everything we do and say today, so that we can set a good example for other people. Amen

41 Sharing together

Before you start

Prepare a range of treats on paper plates, laid out on a table. You could include things like sweets, squares of chocolate, strawberries, grapes, pineapple pieces, carrot sticks, raisins and yogurt in a tube (open at one end). To make the game more difficult, bring some bulky clothes or costumes to dress up in—for example, a big coat, gloves, a hat, sunglasses, an adult onesie, and a mask.

Also bring to the assembly three sets of chopsticks.

Opener: Sharing is fun

Explain that you're going to invite some volunteers to come and eat some of the snacks. But there's a catch. They can't feed themselves; they will have to feed each other. Not only that, but they've got to use chopsticks, and, if they want to make it even more difficult, they can put on some extra clothes.

Invite volunteers to come and take part, and let everyone watch the ensuing chaos. When you have finished the game, ask the children what it was like to try to feed someone else or to be fed?

Thought for the day

Although it's fun to learn to do things for ourselves, it can also be fun to share together. It might not have been the tidiest, most effective way to eat, but there was probably some laughter as the children who volunteered tried to feed each other.

What the Bible says

Jesus eats an important meal with his friends

Then came the day of Unleavened Bread on which the Passover lamb had to be sacrificed. Jesus sent Peter and John, saying, 'Go and make preparations for us to eat the Passover.'

'Where do you want us to prepare for it?' they asked.

He replied, 'As you enter the city, a man carrying a jar of water will meet you. Follow him to the house that he enters, and say to the owner of the house, "The Teacher asks: where is the guest room, where I may eat the Passover with my disciples?" He will show you a large room upstairs, all furnished. Make preparations there.'

They left and found things just as Jesus had told them. So they prepared the Passover.

LUKE 22:7–13

Questions

- What did Jesus send Peter and John to do?
- What's the best meal you've ever shared, and why?
- Where was it and who was there?

Reflection

Ask the children to close their eyes and think quietly about what they've heard today.

Prayer

Thank you, Jesus, that you loved to share your life with your friends. Thank you that it's fun to share. Please help us to share generously what we can with other people. Amen

42 Sharing worries

Before you start

Buy six tiny people figures or make your own out of modelling clay. If you wish, give each one a name. Bring them to the assembly in a small felt or fabric bag.

Opener: Mini magical listening people

Explain that you have brought in a set of six 'magical listeners'. They live very comfortably inside your fabric bag, and they come out when you need someone to listen to you—perhaps when you're feeling angry or sad or confused. Bring your magical listeners out one by one and, if you've named them, tell the children their names, and explain that they are very good at listening. They take away your worries and keep them in their bag, so that you don't have to think about them any more.

Ask the children if anyone would like to borrow a magical listener for a moment and whisper to it something that's been worrying them. Hand out the mini-people to any volunteers, and allow the children time and space to whisper to them before gathering them back in.

As you gather the figures in, tell the children that the magic listeners are keeping their special secrets very safe and won't share them with anyone else, unless the children want them to. Say that the magic listeners are very happy that the children trusted them enough to tell them their worries. They like to help other people by listening. They like it when you share your thoughts and feelings with them, and they promise to look after them.

Now ask the children to think quietly to themselves about who they talk to when they're angry, sad or confused. Who do they share their worries with?

Thought for the day

We all need someone to talk to—someone who will listen to us. Christians believe that God listens to us and really helps take our worries away, if we share them. God cares about us more than the most caring person we can imagine. Isn't that great to know?

What the Bible says

God likes to help people

The righteous cry out, and the Lord hears them; he delivers them from all their troubles.

PSALM 34:17

Questions

- What do we do when we are worried?
- Do we share our worries or keep them to ourselves? Why?
- What does this reading suggest we could do?

Reflection

Ask the children to close their eyes and think quietly about what they've heard today.

Prayer

Thank you, Jesus, that you listen to us whenever we talk to you. Help us to be good listeners too, with our families, our friends, our teachers and each other. Amen

43 Staying healthy

Before you start

Prepare a board with the eight words listed below written on it. Cover each individual letter with a separate sticky note or card.

- Sleep
- Food
- Water
- Hygiene
- Exercise
- Safety
- Clean places
- Health care

Opener: Staying healthy quiz

Ask: Who is feeling well today? Who isn't feeling so well? Who looks after us when we don't feel well?

Ask the children what we need to stay healthy. Point to the words on the board. Uncover the first letter of each word. Ask the children if they can guess what each word is, as you gradually reveal the letters underneath the sticky notes or card.

Explain that we need all these things to be healthy. We need enough sleep, nutritious food, water, good hygiene and exercise every day. We also need to feel safe, to live and learn in clean places and be able to get good health care when we are ill.

Thought for the day

We are very lucky that we have most of the things we need to be healthy. Not every child in the world is so lucky. It's good to remember them and to help them, perhaps by giving money to charity and praying for them.

What the Bible says

Jesus announces that he has come to make people better

[Jesus] went to Nazareth, where he had been brought up, and on the Sabbath day he went into the synagogue, as was his custom. He stood up to read, and the scroll of the prophet Isaiah was handed to him. Unrolling it, he found the place where it is written:

'The Spirit of the Lord is on me, because he has anointed me to proclaim good news to the poor. He has sent me to proclaim freedom for the prisoners and recovery of sight for the blind, to set the oppressed free, to proclaim the year of the Lord's favour.'

LUKE 4:16–19

Questions

Ensure that the children understand any difficult words, such as 'synagogue' (the Jewish place of worship), 'anoint' (to put oil on someone; also suggests a seal of approval), 'oppressed' (having a hard time) and 'proclaim' (to announce or say something out loud).

- What did Jesus say he is going to do?
- Why do you think his words were good news for the people listening to him?

Reflection

Ask the children to close their eyes and think quietly about what they've heard today.

Prayer

Thank you, Jesus, that you care about people being well. You love to make people feel better. Thank you that you are able to heal people. If there are people we know who aren't well, please touch them and be with them. Amen

44 Stronger together

Before you start

Bring to assembly enough paper chain strips for the children to have one each. Hand them out, with pencils, as children enter the hall.

Opener: Let me tell you a story

Read out the following story.

There was a man who was very hungry: he hadn't eaten for several days. He saw that there were fish in the shallows of the sea and decided to try to catch one. He had nothing to catch the fish with, so he just used his hands. All day he tried to catch a fish, but every time he came near to one, it swam away.

The man didn't sleep well because he was so hungry. The next day he was about to try again to catch a fish when a stranger appeared. Quickly, he scrambled to his feet. Was this stranger a friend or enemy? The man held out a hand to him. 'Don't worry,' he said. 'I can see that you are hungry and tired. Let me help you to catch some food.'

All day long, the two tried to catch a fish with the stranger's spear, but every time they tried, the fish escaped under nearby rocks or into seaweed. Evening came and still they had caught nothing.

'Don't worry,' said the stranger. 'I will go to my village, which is not far away, and bring my friends. With their help, I know we will catch some fish to eat.'

The man wasn't sure the stranger was right. Hadn't they tried all day and been unsuccessful? He wasn't sure more spears would make their chances any better. He slept badly again that night, as he was even more hungry than before.

Next morning, the stranger arrived with a group of friends. To the man's surprise, he couldn't see any more spears. 'But what are we going to fish with?' he asked. Laughing, the stranger pointed out a net that his friends had brought. 'We will fish together, using this net. None of us will be hungry by nightfall.'

Sure enough, working together using the net, the man, the stranger and his friends managed to catch not one, not two, but 20 fish that day. They built a huge fire to cook their fish on, and started to celebrate. Not one of them went to bed hungry that night, and the man slept peacefully, comfortable and well-fed among his new friends.

Now ask the children: what made the fishing successful? If the man had remained by himself, what would have happened to him?

Thought for the day

Ask the children to write their name on their paper chain strip and then link it up with the person on either side of them, to make one long paper chain. Explain that we are all stronger together, just like the long paper chain and the friends in the story.

What the Bible says

How we can work together

As it is, there are many parts, but one body. The eye cannot say to the hand, 'I don't need you!' And the head cannot say to the feet, 'I don't need you!' … But God has put the body together, giving greater honour to the parts that lacked it, so that there should be no division in the body, but that its parts should have equal concern for each other. If one part suffers, every part suffers with it; if one part is honoured, every part rejoices with it. Now you are the body of Christ, and each one of you is a part of it.

1 CORINTHIANS 12:20–21, 24B–27

Questions

- What would happen if your eye started arguing with your foot? Or your hand with your elbow?
- What do you think this passage is saying?
- How can we all work together like parts of the body?

Reflection

Ask the children to close their eyes and think quietly about what they've heard today.

Prayer

Thank you, Jesus, that we don't have to do things by ourselves. Thank you that you care for us. Help us to remember that if we work together, even though we may be different, we can do much more than we can do alone. Amen

45 Superheroes

Before you start

Prepare a slideshow presentation of a range of amazing animals that have particular abilities or skills. You could include animals like the lizard or gecko (able to run up walls), puffer fish (able to inflate itself in defence), chameleon (able to disguise itself in any situation), snake (able to slither on its tummy), lion (able to run very fast), eagle (able to see things from a long way away), bat (able to navigate by sonar), hummingbird (able to stay in the air in one place), electric eel (able to use electric shocks on enemies), octopus (able to escape from very small places), and flea (able to jump 100 times its own height).

Opener: What makes it special?

Show the slideshow to the children and ask them to identify the special properties of each animal.

Now ask them to imagine what it would be like to be a human with those abilities. What name could they give to a superhero who had those abilities? (Examples might be Flea Man, Gecko Girl, Chameleo Boy, The Eagle Eyesight and Octo Ninja.)

Thought for the day

If God created all these animals, what might that tell us about what God is like? Christians believe that God created us, too, so we have special powers, like being a good listener, being kind, being funny or being sporty.

What the Bible says

The donkey, the ox and the ostrich

Who let the wild donkey go free? Who untied its ropes? I gave it the wasteland as its home, the salt flats as its habitat. It laughs at the commotion in the town; it does not hear a driver's shout. It ranges the hills for its pasture and searches for any green thing.

Will the wild ox consent to serve you? Will it stay by your manger at night? Can you hold it to the furrow with a harness? Will it till the valleys behind you? Will you rely on it for its great strength? Will you leave your heavy work to it? Can you trust it to haul in your grain and bring it to your threshing-floor?

The wings of the ostrich flap joyfully, though they cannot compare with the wings and feathers of the stork. She lays her eggs on the ground and lets them warm in the sand, unmindful that a foot may crush them, that some wild animal may trample them. She treats her young harshly, as if they were not hers; she cares not that her labour was in vain, for God did not endow her with wisdom or give her a share of good sense. Yet when she spreads her feathers to run, she laughs at horse and rider.

JOB 39:5–18

Questions

Tell the children that, in this reading, God was explaining some things about nature to someone.

- What animals are mentioned in the reading?
- What's your favourite of these animals, and why?
- What special abilities do these animals have? (For example, the ostrich is faster at running than a horse.)

Reflection

Ask the children to close their eyes and think quietly about what they've heard today.

Prayer

Thank you, Jesus, that there are so many amazing creatures in the world. It's fun to find out about them all. Thank you, too, that I have special abilities and skills. Help me to use what's special about me for my benefit and for the benefit of other people too. Amen

46 The importance of books

Before you start

Bring to assembly your favourite book or a pile of books that you particularly like.

Opener: What's your favourite book?

Ask the children if they have a favourite book. What's it about? Who's in it and what happens?

Spend some time talking about your favourite book—or read it out, if it's short. You could even come to assembly dressed as a favourite book character and ask the children to guess who you are.

Ask the children: why do we read? Answers could include: it helps us to learn, it's fun, it's a way to relax, and it's a way to find out information.

Explain that although we have lots of access to books—at school, in our libraries and at home, too—all over the world there are children who cannot get books to read. In schools across the world, there are children who don't have the kind of books we take for granted. They probably don't have books at home, so no one reads them a bedtime story—not because they don't want to, but because books are very expensive and they can't afford them.

Ask the children: what would happen if you didn't have any books to read? Answers could include:

- We wouldn't be able to learn as quickly.
- We wouldn't be able to read to relax.
- We might not be able to find the information we need.

Ask the children to imagine a school with no books. What would it be like?

You could encourage the school or children to consider donating books to other countries, through international schemes such as Bookaid.

Thought for the day

We're very lucky that we have so many books to choose from here, and that we can read for all kinds of reasons. It's good not to take our books for granted.

What the Bible says

Words can help us to see what to do

Your word is a lamp for my feet, a light on my path.

PSALM 119:105

Questions

Explain that Christians believe that the Bible is a very important book.

- Why is a lamp helpful?
- Why might you need a light on your path?
- Why might a book be like that for someone?

Reflection

Ask the children to close their eyes and think quietly about what they've heard today.

Prayer

Thank you, Jesus, that you gave us a very special book, called the Bible. Thank you that it helps to show us how to live our lives in the very best way possible. Thank you that it tells us about you and your love for us. We thank you for the gift of books. Amen

47 The nativity

Before you start

Prepare a visual display of photos of celebrities, as they look now and when they were babies. (You could do an internet search for 'celebrities as babies'.)

Opener: Guess who?

Show the children the display of celebrity baby photos and ask them to guess who they are.

Then ask the children if any of them have a younger brother or sister. If you like, you could also ask any siblings in assembly to stand up, and invite the other children to guess who is related to whom.

Thought for the day

It's exciting when a brand new person is born into the world. Jesus' birth was especially exciting.

What the Bible says

Jesus is born

In those days Caesar Augustus issued a decree that a census should be taken of the entire Roman world. (This was the first census that took place while Quirinius was governor of Syria.) And everyone went to their own town to register.

So Joseph also went up from the town of Nazareth in Galilee to Judea, to Bethlehem the town of David, because he belonged to the house and line of David. He went there to register with Mary, who was pledged to be married to him and was expecting a child. While they were there, the time came for the baby to be born, and she gave birth to her firstborn, a son. She wrapped him in cloths and placed him in a manger, because there was no guest room available for them.

And there were shepherds living out in the fields nearby, keeping watch over their flocks at night. An angel of the Lord appeared to them, and the glory of the Lord shone around them, and they were terrified. But the angel said to them, 'Do not be afraid. I bring you good news that will cause great joy for all the people. Today in the town of David a Saviour has been born to you; he is the Messiah, the Lord. This will be a sign to you: you will find a baby wrapped in cloths and lying in a manger.'

Suddenly a great company of the heavenly host appeared with the angel, praising God and saying, 'Glory to God in the highest heaven, and on earth peace to those on whom his favour rests.'

When the angels had left them and gone into heaven, the shepherds said to one another, 'Let's go to Bethlehem and see this thing that has happened, which the Lord has told us about.'

So they hurried off and found Mary and Joseph, and the baby, who was lying in the manger.

LUKE 2:1–16

Questions

- What's the most exciting news you've ever received?
- In today's reading, what news did the angels bring to the shepherds?
- How do you think the shepherds felt about this news?

Reflection

Ask the children to close their eyes and think quietly about what they've heard today.

Prayer

Thank you, Jesus, that you were born as a human, to be with us and to bring us peace. Thank you for every person here today. We are all special in your eyes. Amen

48 Try something new

Before you start

Bring to assembly five small objects hidden in a drawstring bag.

Opener: What's in the mystery bag?

Invite five volunteers to come to the front.

Ask the first volunteer to put their hand in the bag without looking inside, feel one object in their hand without taking it out of the bag, and try to guess what it is. When they've had a go at guessing, ask them to take the object out to see what it is.

Do the same with the other four volunteers.

Ask the volunteers how it felt to put their hand into the dark bag and try to find an object. Were they excited, nervous, scared or curious? Discuss how it takes courage to try something new and have a go at something, but the experience and the results can be fun.

Thought for the day

Sometimes it can be hard for us to try something new. We don't know how it will work out. But if we can be brave and have a go, we might be surprised by how much fun it is.

What the Bible says

God does new things

Forget the former things; do not dwell on the past. See, I am doing a new thing! Now it springs up; do you not perceive it? I am making a way in the wilderness and streams in the wasteland. The wild animals honour me, the jackals and the owls, because I provide water in the wilderness and streams in the wasteland, to give drink to my people, my chosen, the people I formed for myself that they may proclaim my praise.

ISAIAH 43:18–21

Questions

- Why might it be better to look forward rather than 'dwell on the past'?
- How would you feel if you knew you could trust God with everything that is going to happen?
- Can you think of a 'new thing' you would like to try? Is anything holding you back?

Reflection

Ask the children to close their eyes and think quietly about what they've heard today.

Prayer

Thank you, Jesus, that you are God of the past, present and future. Thank you that you like to do new things. Be with us as we try new things, as we experiment and learn. Thank you that you are with us always, whatever we are doing. Amen

49 Working together

Before you start

Prepare two separate piles of building materials, which the children can see as they come into assembly. Include a range of materials, such as cardboard tubes, paper, card, sticky tape, wool, thread and toilet roll. Also provide child-friendly scissors and glue. Bring to assembly a large timer or a stopwatch and (if you wish) some music to play.

Opener: Build a big tower

Invite ten children to the front and divide them into two teams of five players each. Alternatively, have teams of five children and five teachers.

Explain that you'd like each team to build the biggest tower they possibly can, and that they will have exactly two minutes (or however many minutes you decide) to make their construction. The winner will be the team that builds the tallest tower that can stay upright without any help. Emphasise that their construction will depend on excellent teamwork.

Set a prominent timer that everyone can see, or your stopwatch. Then say, 'On your marks, get set, go!' You could play some music in the background, like the *Mission Impossible* theme, or cartoon music.

When the time is up, call, 'Finish' and ask the volunteers to step away from their constructions.

Declare a winner or, if there isn't an obvious winner, take a vote from the other children in assembly. When you've given the winning team a round of applause, ask everyone to return to their places.

Thought for the day

Teamwork is an essential skill in life, not just in school, and it's important that we learn it.

What the Bible says

The wise men follow a star

Ask the children to think about what dangers, as well as good things, the wise men would have had to face together, and how it would have been vital that they all got on well together. This Bible reading includes their meeting with a very bad king called Herod.

After Jesus was born in Bethlehem in Judea, during the time of King Herod, Magi from the east came to Jerusalem and asked, 'Where is the one who has been born king of the Jews? We saw his star when it rose and have come to worship him.'

When King Herod heard this he was disturbed, and all Jerusalem with him…

Then Herod called the Magi secretly and found out from them the exact time the star had appeared. He sent them to Bethlehem and said, 'Go and search carefully for the child. As soon as you find him, report to me, so that I too may go and worship him.'

After they had heard the king, they went on their way, and the star they had seen when it rose went ahead of them until it stopped over the place where the child was. When they saw the star, they were overjoyed. On coming to the house, they saw the child with his mother Mary, and they bowed down and worshipped him. Then they opened their treasures and presented him with gifts of gold, frankincense and myrrh. And having been warned in a dream not to go back to Herod, they returned to their country by another route.

MATTHEW 2:1–3, 7–12

Questions

- Why did the wise men (or Magi) go to Herod first?
- Why didn't they go back and tell Herod that they had found Jesus?
- How would you have felt if you'd been one of the wise men?
- Do you think it would have been good to be part of a group? Why?

Reflection

Ask the children to close their eyes and think quietly about what they've heard today.

Prayer

Thank you, Jesus, for our friends and the other people who help us to work together. It's good to work together as a team and to share adventures and challenges. Help us to work well with each other, today and every day. Amen

50 World feasts

Before you start

Prepare three plates of different international foods, perhaps related to the children in your school. For example, you could have Jamaican jerk chicken, Indian curry and Polish bread. Arrange the food on three paper plates and keep them hidden from sight as the children come into assembly. Also bring three blindfolds or eye masks.

Opener: Can you guess the food?

Ask for three volunteers who are willing to dare to try something new and who have no food allergies. Ask for three other volunteers to help them. Put the blindfolds or eye masks on the three brave volunteers and ask the other volunteers to guide them into position.

Now bring out the plates of food. Ask the blindfolded children to taste the food and guess what it is. Do they know? When they have finished tasting and guessing, ask the rest of the children if they knew what the food was. Give them the right answers.

Thought for the day

Christians believe that God made the world and it's an amazing place, full of different people and different types of food. God wants us to explore and enjoy new things. Sharing food with different people is a good thing to do.

What the Bible says

The brand new Christians eat together

Those who accepted his message were baptised, and about three thousand were added to their number that day. They devoted themselves to the apostles' teaching and to fellowship, to the breaking of bread and to prayer. Everyone was filled with awe at the many wonders and signs performed by the apostles. All the believers were together and had everything in common. They sold property and possessions to give to anyone who had need. Every day they continued to meet together in the temple courts. They broke bread in their homes and ate together with glad and sincere hearts, praising God and enjoying the favour of all the people.

ACTS 2:41–47

Questions

- What did the new Christians do together?
- Why do you think they shared a special meal together?
- How would you have felt if you'd been at one of their special meals?
- What do you think they might have talked about at the table?

Reflection

Ask the children to close their eyes and think quietly about what they've heard today.

Prayer

Thank you, Jesus, for the gift of food. We're so lucky that we have lots of different kinds of food to choose from in this country. Thank you that we can share our food with each other. Help people who don't have enough food today or who are hungry. Amen

APPENDIX A
Christian festivals and seasons through the year

Here is a list of key Christian festivals and seasons throughout the school year, with suggestions of appropriate assembly outlines from this book.

January
New Year

New Year is celebrated by Christians as a time of new beginnings, looking forward and committing the year to God.

Suggested assemblies:

- Follow the star (18)
- Looking forward (28)
- Try something new (48)

Epiphany

At Epiphany, Christians remember the visit of the wise men to Jesus. It is traditionally celebrated on 6 January.

Suggested assemblies:

- Follow the star (18)
- Working together (49)

February
Shrove Tuesday

Shrove Tuesday (called 'Mardi Gras' in some parts of the world) is the Tuesday immediately before Ash Wednesday and marks the last day before Lent begins. It is traditionally a time of feasting and celebration, before the fasting that accompanies Lent. In the UK it is often a day to eat pancakes.

Suggested assemblies:

- Celebrating (14)
- Sharing together (41)
- World feasts (50)

Ash Wednesday

Ash Wednesday marks the first day of Lent, a season lasting six weeks, leading up to the biggest Christian festival of the year, which is Easter. Many Christians go to church on Ash Wednesday. At some Ash Wednesday services, people are marked on the forehead with ash in the form of the cross.

Suggested assemblies:

- Asking for forgiveness (2)
- Falling out and making up (16)

Lent

Lent lasts for six weeks and leads to Easter. It is traditionally a time of reflection, saying sorry to God, asking for forgiveness, making amends, doing good for others and fasting. It is often seen as a time of preparation and improvement.

Suggested assemblies:

- Asking for forgiveness (2)
- Being kind to each other (8)
- Copying good behaviour (15)
- Falling out and making up (16)
- Good choices (21)
- Keeping going (24)
- Making mistakes (29)
- Setting a good example (40)

Note: the exact dates of Shrove Tuesday, Ash Wednesday and Lent vary from year to year, as they are dependent on the date of Easter.

March
Lent

Lent continues or may even start in March, depending on when Easter Sunday occurs. Suggested assemblies are listed under 'February'.

Palm Sunday

Palm Sunday commemorates the entrance of Jesus into Jerusalem, before he was crucified, and is celebrated on the Sunday before Easter Day. Traditional Christian services include the blessing of palm branches made into the shape of the cross. This is because, according to the Bible, Jesus rode into Jerusalem on a donkey (symbolising humility) and people threw palm branches (symbolising kingship) in his path.

Suggested assemblies:

- Being courageous (3)
- Role models (38)

April

Good Friday

Good Friday is the day when Christians remember the crucifixion and suffering of Jesus. It is a very serious and solemn day in the Christian calendar, as it commemorates Jesus' sacrifice of his own life on the cross to save the world. It takes place on the Friday immediately before Easter Day.

Suggested assemblies:

- Anti-bullying (1)
- Being courageous (3)
- Making mistakes (29)
- Prejudice (35)
- Saying goodbye (39)

Easter Day

Easter Day is a day of great joy in the Christian calendar. It is always on a Sunday, two days after Good Friday. It commemorates Jesus' resurrection from the dead and celebrates new life and hope. Many Christians celebrate Easter Day by going to church and sharing special meals with family and friends. Traditionally, the Easter season lasts a few weeks after Easter Day, just as Lent lasted for a few weeks before Easter Day.

Suggested assemblies:

- Being friends (4)
- Celebrating (14)
- Family (17)
- Laughing is good for you (26)
- World feasts (50)

May

Mary, Jesus' mother

For some Christians, particularly in Europe, May is a month that especially commemorates Mary, the mother of Jesus.

Suggested assemblies:

- Family (17)
- Home (23)
- Mother's Day: mums and carers (32)
- Mother's Day: people who help (33)

June

Whitsun/Pentecost

Whitsun (short for 'Whitsunday'), also known as Pentecost, is a Christian feast that celebrates the gift of the Holy Spirit to Jesus' first followers and to the church. The Holy Spirit is seen by Christians as being the giver of special gifts and talents, including qualities like joy, peace, courage and patience, as well as helping Christians to live good lives and do good for others.

Suggested assemblies:

- Being courageous (3)
- Being friends (4)
- Being inclusive (6)
- Being kind to each other (8)
- Being ourselves (9)
- Gifts and talents (19)
- Laughing is good for you (26)
- Respecting others (36)
- Rest and relaxation (37)
- Staying healthy (43)

September and October

Harvest

September and October have traditionally been times in the Christian calendar to celebrate harvest and give thanks for God's generosity.

Suggested assemblies:

- Being outdoors (10)
- Being thankful (12)
- Planting seeds (34)
- World feasts (50)

November

All Saints

The beginning of November is a time when some Christians celebrate All Saints' Day—a day to honour inspirational Christians from the past, who led by example and lived out a true Christian faith, whether by the courage they showed, by caring for the vulnerable, working in medicine, teaching or helping other people in some way, or by strenuous prayer.

Suggested assemblies:

- Being courageous (3)
- Being ourselves (9)
- Copying good behaviour (15)
- Gifts and talents (19)
- Role models (38)
- Setting a good example (40)
- Stronger together (44)

December

Advent

The whole of December is given over, in the Christian calendar, to Advent. Advent literally means 'coming', and the season is a time that looks forward to the great feast of Christmas. Advent is a time of joy and preparation, when we get ready for Christmas—buying presents, preparing food and paying special attention to prayer and reading the Bible.

Suggested assemblies:

- Being patient (11)
- Celebrating (14)
- Meeting angels (30)

St Nicholas' Day

St Nicholas' Day occurs during Advent, on 6 December. It is an important celebration for European Christians. The day commemorates the figure of St Nicholas, who, it is said, gave out special gifts to people who were poor. For some Christians, St Nicholas is a figure like Santa Claus—someone who gives out presents in secret. Some Christians mark the day with gift giving.

Suggested assemblies:

- Being friends (4)
- Being inclusive (6)
- Being kind to each other (8)
- Home (23)
- Role models (38)
- Sharing together (41)
- Superheroes (45)

Christmas Day

Christmas Day is a day of great celebration in the Christian calendar, as well as being a national holiday in the UK. This day celebrates the birth of Jesus into the world and the beginning of new life. Many Christians attend special church services on this day and celebrate at home with family and friends. You may wish to focus on this in the last week of term, before the Christmas holidays.

Suggested assemblies:

- Being friends (4)
- Sharing together (41)
- The nativity (47)
- World feasts (50)

APPENDIX B
Significant events in the school year

Here are some popular events that are often marked in the school year, and some general themes for you to consider as you plan your assembly schedule. This represents another way that you could divide up the material in this book. Many of the assemblies are flexible and can be used for different themes, but you won't need to repeat an assembly in the same school year.

January

Appropriate themes are new year, beginnings, new year's resolutions and looking for guidance. Focus on starting the year well.
  Suggested assemblies:

- Caring for each other (13)
- Follow the star (18)
- Looking forward (28)
- Role models (38)
- Sharing worries (42)
- Try something new (48)
- Working together (49)

February

Appropriate themes are Valentine's Day, love and family. Focus on relationships.
  Suggested assemblies:

- Being friends (4)
- Being inclusive (6)
- Caring for each other (13)
- Family (17)
- Home (23)

March

Appropriate themes are World Book Day, reading and spring. Focus on learning and growing.
  Suggested assemblies:

- Growing and learning (22)
- Planting seeds (34)
- Staying healthy (43)
- The importance of books (46)

April

Appropriate themes are the middle of the school year and working together. Focus on working as a team.
  Suggested assemblies:

- Being good listeners (5)
- Being inclusive (6)
- Being thankful (12)
- Learning from each other (27)
- Respecting others (36)
- Sharing worries (42)
- Working together (49)

May

Appropriate themes are friendship, what to do when things go wrong and looking after each other in the school family. Focus on friendship.
  Suggested assemblies:

- Anti-bullying (1)
- Asking for forgiveness (2)
- Being friends (4)
- Being kind to each other (8)
- Being ourselves (9)
- Caring for each other (13)
- Falling out and making up (16)
- Good choices (21)
- Meeting angels (30)

June

Appropriate themes are summer, sport, outdoor activities and tests season. Focus on staying healthy.
  Suggested assemblies:

- Being friends (4)
- Being outdoors (9)
- Laughing is good for you (26)
- Rest and relaxation (37)
- Staying healthy (43)

July

Appropriate themes are summer holidays, transition and leavers. Focus on relaxation.
Suggested assemblies:

- Being friends (4)
- Being outdoors (10)
- Going on holiday (20)
- Learning from each other (27)
- Looking forward (28)
- Rest and relaxation (37)
- Saying goodbye (39)

September

Appropriate themes are new school year, standards, behaviour and expectations. Focus on how we treat each other.
Suggested assemblies:

- Being kind to each other (8)
- Caring for each other (13)
- Copying good behaviour (15)
- Good choices (21)
- Making mistakes (29)
- Respecting others (36)
- Setting a good example (40)
- Stronger together (44)

October

Appropriate themes are Black history month, autumn and harvest. Focus on international issues.
Suggested assemblies:

- Being courageous (3)
- More than enough (31)
- Prejudice (35)
- Role models (38)
- Sharing together (41)
- World feasts (50)

November

Appropriate themes are anti-bullying month, caring for others, treating others as we want to be treated and Remembrance. Focus on setting a good example.
Suggested assemblies:

- Anti-bullying (1)
- Being good listeners (5)
- Being thankful (12)
- Copying good behaviour (15)
- Growing and learning (22)
- Keeping going (24)
- Prejudice (35)
- Respecting others (36)
- Role models (38)
- Setting a good example (40)
- Sharing worries (42)

December

Appropriate themes are Christmas, holidays and gifts. Focus on celebrations.
Suggested assemblies:

- Being friends (4)
- Celebrating (14)
- Family (17)
- Gifts and talents (19)
- Laughing is good for you (26)
- Meeting angels (30)
- Rest and relaxation (37)
- Sharing together (41)
- The nativity (47)
- World feasts (50)

About the author

Helen Jaeger teaches in a primary school and is a consultant, journalist and professional creative project manager. She has written twelve books, including *RE in the Classroom with 4–5s* (Barnabas in Schools, 2015).

Enjoyed
this book?

Write a review—we'd love to hear what you think. Email: reviews@brf.org.uk

Keep up to date—receive details of our new books as they happen.
Sign up for email news and select your interest groups at:
www.brfonline.org.uk/findoutmore/

Follow us on Twitter @brfonline

By post—to receive new title information by post (UK only), complete the form below and post to: BRF Mailing Lists, 15 The Chambers, Vineyard, Abingdon, Oxfordshire, OX14 3FE

Your Details
Name _____
Address _____
_____
Town/City _____ Post Code _____
Email _____
Your Interest Groups (*Please tick as appropriate)
☐ Advent/Lent   ☐ Messy Church
☐ Bible Reading & Study   ☐ Pastoral
☐ Children's Books   ☐ Prayer & Spirituality
☐ Discipleship   ☐ Resources for Children's Church
☐ Leadership   ☐ Resources for Schools

Support your local bookshop
Ask about their new title information schemes.